30-minute
vegetarian

30-minute vegetarian

rose elliot

Collins

Contents

Introduction

Welcome to *30-minute Vegetarian.* Whether you're a fully signed-up vegetarian or vegan, a 'flexitarian', 'meat-reducer', 'pescatarian', demi-veg, or just want to enjoy a meat-free meal now and then, come on in. If you want fast, easy, tasty vegetable-based meals; if you're looking for quick meals made from clean, natural, healthy ingredients; if you love exciting flavours, bold colours, vibrant ingredients, eating well and having fun in the kitchen, this is the book for you.

With study after study showing the health benefits of vegetarian food, the World Health Organisation recommending we eat 'five a day', the wealth of amazing vegetables, fruits, grains, pulses, herbs and spices now available from all over the world, and restaurants becoming increasingly creative with their veggie choices, there's never been a better time to try more vegetable-based meals: vegetarian cookery has come of age!

It hasn't always been like this. When, at the tender age of 17, I started cooking vegetarian meals for visitors to the retreat centre run by my family, things were very different. The great majority of visitors had never eaten vegetarian food before. I had to struggle to convince people that they wouldn't fade away or make themselves ill if they gave up meat; I was also up against a much more rigid approach to meals than we have now. 'What on earth do you eat instead of a roast for Sunday dinner?' people used to ask, and the vegetables and ingredients available were very limited: it's hard to believe now that a green pepper was about as exotic as it got, and olive oil was something you bought from the chemist!

In spite of all that, I loved the challenge of creating colourful, tasty food that would please and excite the visitors. I must have done something right, because they raved about the dishes and wanted to know how to make them. So I wrote a recipe book, *Simply Delicious*, published by my family in the autumn of 1967. I thought that it would be a small charity publication that might raise funds for the retreat centre, but it took off immediately, sold out, and was reprinted many times. *Simply Delicious* was, in fact, one of only two vegetarian cookery books on sale nationwide at that time. I must admit to feeling proud that, as far as I am aware, it was the first cookbook ever to stipulate the use of free-range eggs.

I continued to cook at the retreat centre and in 1972 wrote another recipe book, *Not Just a Load of Lentils*, which my family also published, with the practical, spiral binding I wanted. Then things took an unexpected turn: the paperback publisher Fontana (a division of HarperCollins, then called Collins) spotted the book, bought the paperback rights and became my publishers, as indeed they still are today. Over sixty books followed throughout the seventies, eighties, nineties and beyond, and as the book sales added up to the 4-million mark, so the numbers of vegetarians in the UK grew and grew.

Over that time it's been a joy to see the increasing interest in vegetarian cooking. It's always a thrill when people tell me, as they often do, that because of my books they've become vegetarian, started a restaurant, opened a health shop, or written a book. I also love it when, at just about every book signing or demonstration I do, at least one person approaches me, often with a baby, child or even teenager in tow, saying they were raised on my *Vegetarian Mother and Baby Book*. That book, which has had many reprints and new editions, grew from my own experience of bringing up my three daughters as vegetarians (as I was myself). Now, at the time of writing, I have six grandchildren, also vegetarian.

What everyone is asking for now is vegetable-based meals that can be made quickly and easily, and this book, *30-minute Vegetarian*, is my answer. There are 140 recipes ranging from fast starters and snacks, wonderful soups, to luxurious, indulgent desserts, with main courses for every occasion and lots of exciting side dishes too. I've arranged the mains according to how we like to eat them at home, so there's a section of everyday suppers, and another of meals for friends and family ... mix and match as much as you like, add to them, put your own stamp on them, enjoy them.

All the recipes can be made in 30 minutes, some in much less time, others just within the time frame. I admit it: I've pushed it to the limit in a handful of recipes, relying on advance preparation of the ingredients before starting the timer in order to get them done. I hope you'll bear with me on these: they are all special, worth that extra bit of preparation time, and I really wanted you to have them.

I hope you will enjoy making and eating all the dishes as much as I have enjoyed creating, tasting and testing them: have fun, have a feast, celebrate!

Cook's notes

Measurements
Both metric and imperial measurements are given for the recipes.
Use one set of measurements only, not a mixture of the two.

Oven and grill
Preheat the oven to the specified temperature; if using a fan-assisted oven,
follow the manufacturer's instructions for adjusting the temperature.
This usually means reducing the temperature by 20°C (65°F). Grills also
need to be preheated.

Ingredients
As a general rule, buy the best ingredients you can afford on the day.
Prefer 'whole' products, such as wholemeal flour and brown rice, over
more highly processed ones. Look at labels. A good rule of thumb is the fewer
and simpler ingredients in the list the better: no preservatives, stabilisers,
emulsifiers and so on, and nothing with an unpronounceable name!

Always wash vegetables before use. Leaves intended for a salad need to be
dried after being washed, such as in a salad spinner, so excess water doesn't
spoil the final dish.

The recipes in this book are purposely low in sugar; I prefer to use brown
rice syrup (from good wholefood shops) or maple syrup for sweetness. For
seasoning I use sea salt and freshly ground black pepper, either coarse or fine.

For these recipes, use medium eggs (free-range, of course) unless
otherwise stated.

Cheese and dairy
Cheese was traditionally made using rennet taken from the stomachs of
slaughtered calves; some cheeses, such as Parmesan, Gorgonzola, most
Gruyères and Roquefort, still are. However, for most cheeses there are
vegetarian versions, made using rennet derived from plant sources. These
include hard Italian cheeses, often in the economy ranges of supermarkets,
which can easily replace Parmesan. Read the packets, or ask at the cheese
counter for advice. Note that most bought pesto contains Parmesan and is
therefore not vegetarian, but vegetarian and vegan versions are available.
When buying soft cheeses and yoghurts, look out for the addition of gelatine
in some; these, of course, are not vegetarian.

Flavourings

Worcestershire sauce and most Thai pastes contain fish paste; vegetarian versions are available. As always, it's important to read the label. The soy sauce I use is Clearspring's Japanese shoyu soy; according to the label, it's 'made to a traditional recipe using whole soya beans and aged in cedarwood kegs over two summers'. Soy sauces range in quality as much as wine. It can make a great difference to a dish, so buy the best.

Alcohol

Many alcoholic drinks on sale in pubs and on the high street have been made using animal products to clear them of cloudiness in a process called 'fining'. Products used include gelatine, egg white, fish oil, and shells of lobsters and crabs. However, alternative finings are available and there are many wines and other alcoholic drinks that are vegetarian and vegan. Sometimes the labels will tell you this; otherwise, wine merchants and the internet are useful sources of information.

Vegan recipes

Many of the recipes in this book are naturally vegan and are labelled as such. Many more can easily be made vegan by the slight changes suggested below the recipe in *'**Make it vegan**'*.

Soups & Starters

Chilled Beetroot Soup
with Horseradish Cream

One of my all-time favourite soups: I just love the brilliant colour, the sweet-salty balance of the beetroot and seasoning, the little sour hint of lemon, the spiciness of the black pepper ... and for me, it has to be chilled. So that means dicing the vegetables small so they cook quickly, in the minimum amount of water, then cooling the soup rapidly with icy water, in order to get it done in 30 minutes. That's perfectly possible, and it's delicious with its swirl of peppery horseradish cream and cooling green dill leaves.

Serves 4

700ml (1¼ pints) water, put in the freezer or fridge to chill

700g (1½lb) cooked beetroot (without vinegar), roughly diced, chilled in a large bowl in the fridge

1 large onion, finely chopped

1 large potato, peeled and cut into tiny dice: not more than 5mm (¼in)

1 tbsp olive oil

500ml (18fl oz) boiling water

Zest and juice of ½ lemon

Salt and black pepper

A few sprigs of fresh dill, to serve

For the horseradish cream

6 tbsp single cream

1–2 tbsp horseradish sauce or relish from a jar

1. Put the water and beetroot in the fridge to chill. It's a good idea to put soup bowls into the fridge at the same time; the cooler everything is, the faster the soup can be made.

2. Fry the onion and potato in the oil in a large saucepan, without browning, for 7–10 minutes.

3. Add the boiling water and lemon zest, and leave to simmer over a gentle heat for about 10 minutes, or until the potato and onions are completely soft.

4. While this is happening, mix the cream with enough of the horseradish cream or relish to give a nice kick; set aside.

5. Tip the potato and onion mixture into the chilled bowl of beetroot from the fridge and process with a hand-held blender until silky smooth. Stir in the icy water from the freezer or fridge, then add about 2 tablespoons of lemon juice and season with salt and pepper.

6. To serve, ladle the soup into chilled bowls, swirl with the horseradish cream and finish with some fresh dill.

Make it vegan: Use soya cream and non-dairy horseradish relish.

Celeriac Soup with Truffle Oil and Cheese Crisps

Salty, celery-flavoured celeriac makes a wonderful, creamy soup, and when topped with a generous swirl of truffle oil and bits of crunchy, crisped cheese it becomes really special.

Serves 4

1 onion, chopped

1 celeriac, about 700g (1½lb), thickly peeled and cut into 1cm (½in) cubes

1 tbsp olive oil

1.5 litres (2½ pints) water

Salt and black pepper

About 4 tbsp truffle oil, to serve

For the cheese crisps

40g (1½oz) freshly grated Parmesan-style cheese

2 tbsp semolina

1. Fry the onion and celeriac in the oil in a large saucepan, covered, for 5 minutes, until beginning to soften.

2. Pour in 1 litre (1¾ pints) of the water, bring to the boil, then leave to simmer for about 15 minutes, or until the celeriac is tender.

3. Meanwhile, make the cheese crisps: sprinkle just over half the cheese into a large, dry frying pan, to make a thin, lacy layer. Put the frying pan over a moderate heat for about 30 seconds, until the cheese has melted, then sprinkle 1 tablespoon of the semolina over the top, followed by the rest of the cheese, then the last of the semolina. Leave it for about another minute, until the cheese turns pale golden, then take the pan off the heat and leave the crisp to cool in it. It will crisp as it cools and become easy to lift out of the frying pan with a spatula.

4. Blend the soup until it is smooth and creamy, using a hand-held blender or food processor, and adding the rest of the water as necessary to get the consistency you like. Season with salt and pepper.

5. Serve the soup in bowls, swirl some truffle oil on top, then scrunch some of the cheesy crisp over. Serve at once.

Tip: Real Parmesan cheese is not vegetarian because it is made using animal rennet. However, there are a number of strong or hard vegetarian Italian cheeses you can use instead.

Creamy Swede Soup with Fried Onion and Cumin Topping

Swedes are available all winter, and are cheap as chips, yet what can you do with them to make them taste really delicious? They're good mashed in a half-and-half mix with carrots and also in a vegetable curry, where the spices add zing and interest. Or try them in this delicious soup; it's naturally creamy and delicate, with the onion and cumin topping adding a lovely burst of extra flavour and texture.

Serves 4

Vegan

1 onion, chopped

1 swede, about 700g (1½lb), thickly peeled and cut into 1cm (½in) cubes

1 tbsp olive oil

Cinnamon stick

1.5 litres (2½ pints) water

Salt and black pepper

For the topping

1 onion, sliced

1 tbsp olive oil

1 tsp cumin seeds

1. Fry the onion and swede in the oil in a large saucepan, with the cinnamon stick, covered, for 5 minutes, until beginning to soften.

2. Pour in 1 litre (1¾ pints) of the water, bring to the boil, then leave to simmer for about 15 minutes, or until the swede is tender.

3. Meanwhile, prepare the topping: fry the onion in the oil for about 7 minutes, until tender, then turn up the heat and allow them to brown a bit. Add the cumin seeds for the last couple of minutes of cooking.

4. Blend the soup until it is really smooth and creamy, using a hand-held blender or food processor, and adding the rest of the water as necessary to get the consistency you like. Season with salt and pepper.

5. Serve the soup in bowls, each topped with a spoonful of the onion and cumin mixture.

Tip: This soup is also lovely made with parsnips instead of swedes.

Tuscan Bean Soup

You can't beat this on a cold day with some good crusty bread, and it's so quick and easy to make. You can vary the beans: borlotti are excellent, too.

Serves 4

Vegan

2 tbsp olive oil

2 onions, chopped

4 garlic cloves, crushed

2 × 400g tins cannellini beans

About 400ml (14fl oz) water or vegetable stock

1 lemon, halved

Salt and black pepper

Extra virgin olive oil, to serve (optional)

Roughly chopped flat-leaf parsley, to serve

1. Heat the oil in a large saucepan, add the onions then cover and cook gently for 10 minutes, until tender but not brown. Stir in the garlic and cook for 1–2 minutes longer.

2. Add the cannellini beans, together with their liquid, then purée in a food processor or with a hand-held blender until fairly smooth and creamy.

3. Return the mixture to the pan and add some water or vegetable stock to adjust the consistency to your liking. Bring to the boil, then season with salt and pepper and a squeeze or two of lemon juice to bring out the flavour.

4. Serve the soup in warmed bowls, topped with a drizzle of extra virgin olive oil, if you like, some flat-leaf parsley and coarsely ground black pepper.

Butternut Squash Soup with Chilli Oil

When it comes to making soup, you can't get much simpler than this, yet it is one of the most delectable soups of all. There are two ways of making it: to keep within 30 minutes, I'm giving the top-of-the-stove version, but you can also roast the butternut squash instead (see the tip below), and whilst this takes around 1 hour, if you roast the squash in advance, perhaps when you've got the oven on for something else, this soup can be made in about 10 minutes.

Serves 4

Vegan

2 tbsp olive oil

1 butternut squash, weight about 1kg (2lb 2oz), peeled and cut into 1cm (½in) cubes

About 750ml (27fl oz) vegetable stock, made with 1 tsp stock powder

Salt and black pepper

Chilli oil, to serve

1. Heat the oil in a large saucepan and add the butternut squash cubes. Cook, covered, over a gentle heat for 10 minutes, until the butternut squash is softening, stirring from time to time: don't let it get brown.

2. Add 500ml (18fl oz) of the stock, bring to the boil, and simmer until the squash is tender: about 15 minutes.

3. Blend the soup with a hand-held blender or in a food processor until smooth. Add more stock if necessary to get the consistency you like; reheat as necessary. Season with salt and pepper.

4. Ladle the soup into warm bowls, swirl with chilli oil, and serve.

Tip: To roast a butternut squash, pierce it with a skewer or pointed knife in several places, rub the skin all over with olive oil and bake it in a roasting tin at 190ºC (375ºF), Gas 5 for about 1–1¼ hours, or until you can easily pierce it with a knife. Cool, or use straight away, as you please. To make the soup, open up the squash, remove the seeds, strings and stalk end, then whizz the pieces of squash in a food processor, or in a pan, with a hand-held blender, until smooth. Proceed with the recipe as above, from the point at which you add the water. If you use an organic butternut squash, and have a good blender, it's fine to include the skin when you purée it.

Green Pea and Mint Soup

If you're looking for a quick soup this one is hard to beat. Although it can be made all year round, it has a refreshing summery flavour.

Serves 4

15g (½oz) butter

1 onion, chopped

125g (4½oz) potato, diced

450g (1lb) frozen petits pois

4–5 sprigs of mint

About 1 litre (1¾ pints) vegetable stock, made with 1–2 tsp stock powder

Salt and black pepper

1 lemon, halved

1. Melt the butter in a large saucepan and gently fry the onion and potato for about 10 minutes.

2. Add the petits pois, the leaves from the mint sprigs and most of the stock. Bring to the boil, then simmer gently for 10–15 minutes or until the potato and onion are tender.

3. Blend the soup, then pour it through a sieve back into the pan. Thin with a little extra water if you like, then reheat gently. Season well with salt and pepper and a good squeeze of lemon juice.

Mango and Red Chilli Salad

A luscious marriage of contrasting colours, flavours and textures: soft, sweet mango with sharp, fragrant lime, a kick of red chilli, a crunch of salty roasted cashew nuts, a few lettuce and wild rocket leaves. Easy to make, pretty to look at, lovely to eat.

Serves 2

Vegan

1 large, juicy mango

1 lime

½ mild red chilli or a few pinches of dried red chilli flakes

A few leaves from a round lettuce

2 handfuls wild rocket leaves

50g (2oz) salted roasted cashew nuts

1. Cut the two cheeks of the mango about 5mm (¼in) each side of the stalk; then cut off the peel and cut the flesh into chunky bite-size pieces.

2. Pare the zest of the lime into some long thin strands, using a zester if you have one, or else a fine grater. Squeeze out the juice.

3. Deseed the chilli and cut into thin slices or rounds.

4. Mix the mango chunks with the lime zest and chilli (keeping some slivers of each back to use as decoration) then add enough of the lime juice to make it the right degree of sharpness for you.

5. Place some lettuce and rocket leaves on each serving plate, then arrange the chunks of mango and the cashews on top, to make an attractive, colourful heap, decorating with the reserved lime zest and chilli.

Tip: A zester is a gadget you can buy cheaply from a kitchen shop and is well worth having as you can make lovely thin strands of citrus peel quickly and easily.

Grilled Chicory and Fennel with Tomato Marinade

This shows just how delicious vegetables can be, even when cooked quite simply, and I think it makes a lovely, refreshing first course, or dish for the barbecue. Serve it just as it is, or with some light bread, such as ciabatta, to soak up the delicious garlicky, tomatoey juices.

Serves 4

Vegan

2 fennel, outer bracts shaved with a potato peeler to remove tough strings, halved

4 medium heads of chicory, halved

8 fresh bay leaves

Bunch of fresh dill

½ tsp dill seeds

Sea salt and black pepper

Wedges of lemon, to serve

For the tomato and garlic paste

6 garlic cloves, crushed, or 1 tbsp garlic purée

3 tbsp tomato purée

1 tbsp sun-dried tomato paste

1 tbsp lemon juice

2 tbsp olive oil

½ tsp salt

1. Cook the fennel, cut-side down, in 1cm (½in) boiling water, for 10–15 minutes, until you can pierce it easily with a knife. Drain and rinse in cold water to cool quickly.

2. Meanwhile, make the tomato and garlic paste by mixing all the ingredients together.

3. Spread some of the paste over the fennel and chicory halves, coating them generously. Tuck a fresh bay leaf and sprig of fresh dill between two of the outer leaves of each chicory half.

4. Put some sprigs of dill on a grill pan, or shallow heatproof dish that will fit under your grill, and put the chicory and fennel on top, cut sides towards the heat. Grill for about 12 minutes, until the chicory and fennel are tender and lightly browned.

5. Scatter the fennel and chicory with a few dill seeds, and season with salt and pepper. Serve with some sprigs of dill and lemon wedges.

Tip: You can also cook this on a barbecue: put the vegetables on a fine mesh grid on top of the barbecue, with some fennel leaves on top, and cook until they are lightly browned, about 12 minutes.

Asian Pear Salad

This is such a pretty salad of contrasting colours, flavours and textures. Asian pears have a crisp juiciness and a delicate, slightly savoury flavour. I love them in this salad but you could equally well use ordinary pears: choose the variety you like best, and use them slightly under-ripe and crisp, for a similar texture. If you can't find mizuna, that pretty Asian green with a mustardy taste, rocket or watercress will be fine.

Serves 4

Vegan

1 small/medium radicchio

2 chicory

2 large handfuls of mizuna

2 Asian pears

Handful of black olives

For the dressing

2 tbsp olive oil

2 tbsp balsamic vinegar

¼–½ tsp sea salt

½–1 tsp cracked black pepper

1. Separate the leaves of the radicchio and chicory and arrange them along with the mizuna on individual serving plates.

2. Peel, core and thinly slice the pears and divide between the plates; add a few olives to each plate.

3. Make a dressing by whisking together the oil, vinegar and salt, and drizzle over the plates. Finish each with a little scattering of cracked black pepper, and serve.

Radicchio alla Griglia

You've just got to try this! It's my version of a classic Italian way with radicchio, using lemon, garlic and sun-dried tomato paste to replace the traditional anchovies and make the recipe vegetarian – and it's wonderful, even though I do say it myself … One day, when I couldn't find any radicchio, I tried it with firm little gem lettuces, and they were lovely too. I find bought garlic paste, which larger supermarkets sell with the jars of herbs and spices, time-saving and perfect for this recipe. You'll find jars of sun-dried tomato paste close by, or in tubes with the normal tomato purée. If you can't get walnut oil, then use olive oil. Enough from me: the recipe.

Serves 4

1 large radicchio, quartered,
    or 2 smaller ones, halved
25g (1oz) crushed walnuts, to serve
Flakes of Parmesan-style cheese,
    to serve (optional)

For the tomato and garlic paste

1 tbsp garlic purée
2 tbsp sun-dried tomato paste
2 tbsp freshly squeezed lemon juice
4 tbsp walnut or olive oil
Salt and black pepper

1. First make the paste by mixing all the ingredients together, seasoning with salt and pepper.

2. Spread the paste all over the radicchio sections, pushing it between the leaves and on all the surfaces, covering it completely.

3. Put the radicchio under the grill, or on a fine mesh grid over a barbecue, with the cut edges of the radicchio towards the heat. Grill for about 3 minutes, until the radicchio is beginning to wilt and brown slightly on the edges, then turn the pieces and grill for a further 2–3 minutes or so.

4. While the radicchio is grilling, toast the crushed walnuts by stirring them in a saucepan over a moderate heat for a minute or two until they begin to brown a bit and smell toasty. Tip them out of the pan immediately to prevent burning.

5. Serve the radicchio hot, scattered with the toasted walnuts and flakes of Parmesan-style cheese, if you like.

Roasted Asparagus with Instant Hollandaise

OK, I exaggerate slightly: the sauce isn't totally instant, but it's very fast and easy. When whizzed up in a blender and served with asparagus, it makes a wonderful early summer treat. I love the way that roasting asparagus concentrates the flavour (and is so easy to do) but you could cook it in a little water if you prefer, for 3–4 minutes until just tender. Vegans can enjoy this too: see below for a fabulous vegan mayonnaise.

Serves 4

500g (1lb 2oz) asparagus, trimmed

2 tbsp olive oil

Sea salt

For the hollandaise sauce

250g (9oz) butter, cut into chunks

4 egg yolks

2 tbsp lemon juice

Black pepper

1. Preheat the oven to 220°C (425°F), Gas 7.

2. Toss the asparagus in the olive oil, spread out on a baking sheet, sprinkle with salt, and roast for about 10 minutes, or until just tender and lightly browned in places.

3. Meanwhile, make the hollandaise sauce. Melt the butter gently in a saucepan without browning it. Put the egg yolks, lemon juice and some salt and pepper into a blender or food processor and whizz for 1 minute until the mixture is thick. With the motor running, pour in the melted butter in a thin, steady stream – the sauce will thicken. Let it stand for 1–2 minutes.

4. Serve the asparagus with the sauce either poured over it or put into small ramekins for dipping.

Make it vegan: Creamy tofu mayonnaise is wonderful with the asparagus (and lots of other dishes too). Put the following into a food processor or blender: 200g (7oz) firm tofu (the normal type you can buy in any supermarket), drained; 1½ tbsp cider vinegar; 2 tbsp olive oil; 1 tsp Dijon mustard and ¼ tsp salt, and whizz until smooth. Get it really light and creamy: you'll love it. It keeps for 5 to 7 days in the fridge, so it's good to have on hand.

Grilled Fennel with Goat's Cheese and Olives

The secret to preparing delicious aniseedy fennel is to remove any tough fibres by shaving the outer bracts all round with a swivel-blade peeler – it makes all the difference. I also find that it's best to par-boil fennel before roasting it, so you end up with tender, chunky pieces, nicely charred at the edges.

Serves 4

2 large fennel, shaved down the sides with a swivel-blade peeler to remove tough fibres, then sliced downwards into sixths or eighths

200g (7oz) smooth white goat's cheese

2 tbsp chopped chives

Black or green olives

For the lemon and pepper marinade

4 tbsp olive oil

Zest and juice of ½ lemon

1 garlic clove, crushed

½ tsp sea salt

1 bay leaf, torn in half

½ tsp coarsely ground black peppercorns

1. Cook the fennel in 1cm (½in) boiling water for about 8 minutes, until just tender. Drain.

2. Lay the fennel pieces in a single layer on a grill pan or shallow container that will fit under your grill.

3. Make the marinade by mixing, or whisking, all the ingredients together.

4. Pour the marinade over the fennel pieces, making sure they're all coated, then leave to marinate for at least 10 minutes, or until 10 minutes before you want to eat.

5. Drain off and reserve any excess marinade. Grill the fennel for 5–10 minutes, until charred around the edges.

6. Put the pieces of fennel in a large dish and pour the remaining marinade over them. Serve with soft white goat's cheese, scattered with chopped chives and olives.

Tip: You can also cook this on a barbecue, spreading the pieces out on a fine mesh grid.

Make it vegan: You can make a delicious version of this using bought vegan garlic and herb cream cheese in place of the goat's cheese.

Little Goat's Cheese Filo Parcels with Cranberry Sauce

These are very easy to make, and universally popular. The number of sheets in a packet of filo pastry, and the size of the sheets, vary from brand to brand; don't worry about getting the size of the pieces absolutely exact; near enough will be fine. The recipe makes more cranberry sauce than you'll need for the recipe, but it will keep in the fridge for about 4 weeks or so.

Serves 4–6

1 packet filo pastry, cut into 36 squares, each about 15cm (5in)

Olive oil, for brushing

300g (11oz) smooth white goat's cheese (the kind without rind)

Baby red chard salad leaves, to serve

A little vinaigrette, to serve

For the cranberry sauce

300g (11oz) fresh cranberries

250g (9oz) golden granulated sugar

Juice of ½ orange

1. Preheat the oven to 200ºC (400ºF), Gas 6. Brush a 12-hole shallow bun tin with olive oil.

2. To make a parcel, brush the surface of 3 squares of pastry with olive oil and lay them overlapping each other to form a 12-pointed star shape.

3. Put a good heaped teaspoonful (about 25g/1oz) of goat's cheese in the centre, draw the sides up around it and scrunch them together at the top to form a little parcel. Put it in one of the holes in the bun tin.

4. Repeat with the rest of the filo squares and goat's cheese, to make 12 parcels in all.

5. Make the cranberry sauce. Put the cranberries into a pan with the sugar and orange juice. Cook over a gentle heat for a few minutes until the sugar has dissolved, then simmer for about 10 minutes, or until the cranberries are tender. The mixture will thicken as it cools.

6. Bake the filo pastries for about 10–15 minutes, or until crisp and lightly browned. Serve at once with the cranberry sauce and a leafy salad dressed with vinaigrette.

Make it vegan: Use vegan cream cheese instead of the goat's cheese.

A Trio of Dips

Three easy, popular dips you can rustle up very quickly: perfect for an impromptu snack or party.

Stilton and Port with Black Pepper

Serves 4

200g (7oz) Stilton,
    broken into rough pieces
100g (3½oz) soft cheese
1 tbsp port
Salt and crushed black pepper

This flavour combination is a classic.

Process the Stilton, soft cheese and port to a smooth cream, using a food processor or hand-held blender. Season lightly with salt if necessary, then spoon into a dish and sprinkle generously with crushed black pepper.

Guacamole

Serves 4
Vegan

3 avocados, peeled, stoned
    and cut into rough chunks
Juice of 1 lime
28g bunch fresh coriander,
    roughly chopped
1 red chilli, deseeded and sliced
2–3 tbsp finely chopped red onion
Salt

This is a lovely bright green guacamole, fresh with lime and coriander, and with the crunch of red onion.

Blend the avocado and lime juice to a creamy consistency in a food processor or with a hand-held blender. Add the coriander, then stir in the chilli, red onion, and salt to taste; at this point, you can leave it all chunky, or give it a whirl with the hand-held blender or in the food processor until it's the consistency you like. Serve in a small dish.

Red Pepper Salsa

Serves 4
Vegan

1 red pepper, deseeded and
    roughly chopped
1 red onion, roughly chopped
1–2 tomatoes, roughly chopped
About 1 tbsp tomato ketchup,
    or to taste
Tabasco sauce
Salt

Quick to whizz up, spicy and versatile: this is great as a dip, or can be served with many dishes to bring a refreshing flavour note and a burst of colour.

Blend the red pepper, onion and tomatoes in a food processor or with a hand-held blender until finely chopped. Stir in tomato ketchup to taste – about 1 tablespoon – and season with a drop or two of Tabasco and some salt. Put into a bowl to serve.

Artichoke Hearts with Baby Mushrooms

This is an almost instant starter that you can put together really easily using one of my favourite 'short-cut' ingredients: char-grilled (sometimes called barbecued or roasted) baby artichoke hearts, available in any supermarket, usually in the chiller section with the olives. This is lovely served warm, with some soft, light bread, such as ciabatta, also warm, to mop up the juices.

Serves 4

Vegan

400g (14oz) packet char-grilled artichokes in sunflower oil

300g (11oz) baby button mushrooms, wiped, any large ones halved

2 garlic cloves, crushed

1 bay leaf

2 tbsp freshly squeezed lemon juice

Salt and black pepper

Chopped flat-leaf parsley, to serve

Warm ciabatta bread, to serve

1. Tip the char-grilled artichokes, oil and all, into a large saucepan, and add the mushrooms, garlic and bay leaf. Put the pan over a moderate heat and let the mushrooms cook gently in the oil for about 10 minutes.

2. Stir in the lemon juice, check the seasoning and add salt and pepper as necessary.

3. Divide between 4 warmed plates, scatter with chopped parsley and serve with warm bread.

Little Aubergine Fritters with Caper Sauce

These are deliciously crisp and crunchy on the outside, tender within, and very easy to make. I love them with a creamy caper sauce – one of my absolute favourites.

Serves 4

2 medium-sized aubergines

Olive oil, for shallow-frying

Lemon wedges, to serve

For the coating (see tip below)

120g (4oz) cornflour

½ tsp salt

90–120ml (3½–4½fl oz) water

100g (3½oz) fine dried breadcrumbs

For the caper sauce

4 generous tbsp mayonnaise

1 tbsp capers, chopped

1. Peel the aubergines using a swivel-blade potato peeler; remove the stalks, and cut the aubergines into slices about 8mm (¼in) thick. You can cut them into circles, long slices, fingers or triangles, whatever shape appeals to you.

2. Mix the cornflour, salt and water to make a mixture that is soft enough to dip the aubergine slices into but stiff enough to stick to them; I stir the mixture with my fingers as I add the water gradually so that I can feel when it reaches this stage.

3. Dip the aubergine pieces first in the cornflour mixture, then into the crumbs, to coat them all over.

4. Heat enough olive oil in a frying pan to coat the surface lightly, then put in the fritters and fry them on both sides, until they are crisp, golden brown, and the aubergine inside feels tender when pierced with a sharp pointed knife. Drain them on kitchen paper.

5. While they are frying, quickly make the sauce by mixing together the mayonnaise and capers. Put into a small serving bowl.

6. Serve the fritters with lemon wedges, and the sauce.

Tip: The cornflour-and-crumb coating is my favourite for fritters, croquettes and so on. I find the thin but sticky paste gives a wonderfully reliable, crisp result, which I prefer to an egg-and-breadcrumb coating.

Make it vegan: Instead of dairy mayonnaise, use the Tofu Mayonnaise on page 26.

Figs with Stilton and Warm Honey and Balsamic Dressing

A delicious combination of flavours and colours, this is a perfect autumn – or Christmas – starter, and is very easy to make. Try to get sweet ripe figs if you can, although the balsamic and honey marinade will help along less-than-perfect ones. There are plenty of good vegetarian Stiltons to choose from.

Serves 4

4 fresh ripe figs

8 round lettuce leaves, such as
    outer leaves of little gems

4 small handfuls watercress,
    trimmed

175g (6oz) Stilton, cut or broken
    into bite-size pieces

Black pepper

For the dressing

1 tbsp strongly flavoured honey, such
    as thyme or fair-trade forest honey

1 tbsp olive oil

2 tbsp balsamic vinegar

Good pinch of salt

1. Slice the figs down through the stem into eighths.

2. In a small saucepan, gently heat the honey, olive oil and balsamic vinegar until the honey melts. Mix in the salt, then add the figs, stir gently over the heat for a minute or two until the figs are coated with dressing and slightly warmed. Remove from the heat.

3. Arrange two rounded lettuce leaves on each serving plate; top with watercress, the slices of fig and the Stilton.

4. Drizzle any remaining dressing over the top, grind over some black pepper, and serve.

Snacks &
Light Meals

Warm Lime-roasted Sweet Potato and Couscous Salad

This is both comforting and refreshing; dense, candy-like sweet potato sharpened with lime, the crunch of red onion and the fresh green coriander, against the background of silky couscous. It's lovely on its own, or you could add some sharp goat's cheese or hummus to complete the meal.

Serves 4

Vegan

600g (1lb 6oz) sweet potatoes, about 4 medium-sized ones, scrubbed and cut into 2cm (¾in) chunks

2 tbsp olive oil

500ml (18fl oz) vegetable stock

250g (9oz) couscous

Finely grated zest and juice of 1 lime

4 tbsp finely chopped red onion

14g (½oz) fresh coriander, roughly chopped – or left in sprigs

Salt and black pepper

1. Preheat the oven to 220ºC (425ºF), Gas 7.

2. Toss the sweet potato chunks in 1 tablespoon of the olive oil, put them into a roasting tin, and bake for 25 minutes, turning after 10–15 minutes, until they are tender and golden brown.

3. Meanwhile, bring the vegetable stock to the boil, then add the couscous and the remaining tablespoon of olive oil. Cover and set aside, off the heat, for 10–15 minutes.

4. Take the sweet potatoes out of the oven and toss with the lime zest and juice, the chopped onion and coriander. Season with salt and pepper.

5. Stir the couscous with a fork, and add a little salt, then carefully mix with the sweet potatoes and coriander, and serve.

Bulgur, Edamame, Pea and Broad Bean Salad with Minted Yoghurt Dressing

This is a wonderfully nutritious main course salad that also tastes fresh and summery with its lovely minty dressing. You can find packets of podded edamame beans, looking rather like frozen peas, in large supermarkets and in health shops. They are in fact young, green soya beans, and are high in protein and other nutrients. Some crisp lettuce leaves, and maybe a salad of summer tomatoes and basil (such as the Mixed Heirloom Tomato Salad, page 180), would go really well with this.

Serves 4

200g (7oz) bulgur wheat

400ml (14fl oz) water

100g (3½oz) frozen podded edamame beans, thawed

100g (3½oz) frozen petits pois, thawed

200g (7oz) sugar snap peas, trimmed

150g (5oz) frozen broad beans

6 spring onions, chopped

4 tbsp chopped flat-leaf parsley

2 tbsp extra virgin olive oil

2 tbsp freshly squeezed lemon juice

Salt and black pepper

For the minted yoghurt dressing

300ml (11fl oz) plain yoghurt

2 tbsp chopped mint

1. Put the bulgur wheat into a saucepan with the water. Bring to the boil, put the thawed edamame beans and peas on top, then take off the heat and leave to stand, covered, for 15 minutes, or until the bulgur wheat is fluffy and tender.

2. Meanwhile, cook the sugar snap peas in boiling water until tender, about 3 minutes; remove them with a slotted spoon into a colander (don't throw away the water) and refresh under cold water; set aside.

3. Bring the water in the pan back to the boil and add the broad beans. Cook for 2 minutes; drain, and cool quickly under cold water. I like to pop off their skins with my fingers, to reveal the brilliant green inner beans, but this isn't essential: by all means leave them on, if you prefer.

4. When the wheat is ready, give it a stir with a fork to fluff it and mix in the edamame beans and peas, then add the sugar snap peas, broad beans, chopped spring onions, parsley, olive oil, lemon juice, and salt and pepper to taste.

5. Make the dressing by mixing the yoghurt with the chopped mint, and seasoning with a little salt and pepper. Serve with the bulgur wheat salad, in a small jug or bowl.

Make it vegan: Use plain unsweetened soya yoghurt for the dressing.

Baby Green Bean and Butter Bean Salad with Garlic Croutes

I love the combination of fresh green beans in the pod and cooked dried beans; they are at the same time refreshing and sustaining. This salad is lovely made in the summer with flavourful tomatoes, olives and fresh herbs.

Serves 2–4

Vegan

250g (9oz) thin French beans,
    trimmed as much as you wish
    (see tip below)
400g tin butter beans, drained
250g (9oz) tomatoes,
    plum if available, sliced
Few sprigs of basil, torn
Handful of black olives
Salt and coarsely ground
    black pepper

For the garlic croutes

1 garlic clove
2–4 slices of baguette
    or wholemeal bread
Olive oil

For the mustard dressing

1 tsp Dijon mustard
1 tbsp red wine or cider vinegar
3 tbsp olive oil

1. Cook the beans in boiling water to cover for 4–6 minutes, or until tender but still crunchy. Drain in a colander and cool under the cold tap. Drain again.

2. Put the cooked beans into a bowl and add the butter beans, tomatoes, basil, and olives. Season with salt and a little pepper.

3. Make the garlic croutes: cut the garlic in half and rub the cut surfaces over one side of the slices of bread, then brush the bread lightly on both sides with olive oil. Grill the bread on both sides until lightly browned and crisp.

4. While the bread is grilling, make the dressing: put the mustard, vinegar and a little salt into a bowl and mix with a fork or small whisk, then gradually whisk in the oil. Season.

5. Add half the dressing to the salad and toss so that it's all glossy, then heap it on to plates or a serving dish and drizzle the rest of the dressing over and around, and grind some more pepper coarsely over. Serve with the garlic croutes.

Tip: I've got more and more relaxed about how much I trim beans. I used to cut off both the top and the curly 'tail'; then I just trimmed the top, now I prefer not to trim them at all: I think they look much prettier in their natural state, and of course it's less work for the cook! But others disagree ... so the choice is yours.

Mexican Bean Salad

This is half salad, half hot dish, a variation of Mexican refried beans, with a hot, chilli-bean mixture served on a base of salad, garnished with slices of avocado, soured cream, chives and coriander. You could also add a handful of olives, and some tortilla chips for an extra crunch. It's a great one-dish meal to make when you want something quick, hot and tasty, and it's very colourful.

Serves 2

1 tbsp olive oil

1 onion, chopped

1 green chilli, deseeded and sliced

1 garlic clove, crushed

400g tin chopped tomatoes

400g tin red kidney beans, drained

1 small lettuce

1 small red pepper, deseeded
    and sliced

4 tomatoes, sliced

1 avocado

2 tbsp chopped fresh chives

150ml (5fl oz) plain yoghurt or
    soured cream

Salt and black pepper

A few fresh coriander leaves,
    to serve (optional)

1. Heat the oil in a saucepan, then add the onion, cover and cook over a moderate heat for 5 minutes, stirring occasionally.

2. Add the chilli, garlic and chopped tomatoes to the onion and cook for 5 minutes.

3. Add the beans to the onion mixture, mashing them roughly with a wooden spoon or a potato masher to give a chunky texture. Heat through, then season with salt and pepper and keep warm over a low heat.

4. Cover a large platter with the lettuce leaves and arrange the red pepper and tomatoes randomly on top.

5. Peel, stone and roughly chop the avocado. Stir the chives into the yoghurt or soured cream.

6. Spoon the red bean mixture on to the centre of the salad. Sprinkle the chopped avocado over it, then drizzle some of the yoghurt or soured cream mixture over everything – put the rest into a small bowl to serve with the salad. Serve the salad at once, garnished with fresh coriander leaves, if you wish.

Make it vegan: Replace dairy soured cream or yoghurt with vegan ones: you can get vegan soured cream at health shops and plain, unsweetened soya yoghurt at large wholefood stores.

Warm Quinoa Salad with Broad Beans and Pomegranate

A pretty, refreshing salad that's light but nourishing and can be served warm or cold. I love it just as it is, but you can jazz it up: serve it with crisp little gem lettuce leaves to use as scoops; have it with some salty crumbled feta, some hummus or another of the creamy dips in this book, such as the Tofu Mayonnaise on page 26, and some slices of ripe avocado, or a swirl of Sunflower Cream (see page 148).

Serves 2–4

Vegan

125g (4½oz) quinoa

250ml (9fl oz) water

200g (7oz) frozen broad beans

1 pomegranate

4 slim spring onions, chopped

Salt

For the dressing (optional)

1 tbsp brown rice vinegar

1 tbsp mirin

2 tsp chopped fresh mint

1. Rinse the quinoa in a sieve under the cold tap, then put it into a saucepan with the water, bring to the boil, cover and leave to simmer over a gentle heat for about 15 minutes, until all the water has been absorbed and the quinoa is fluffy.

2. Meanwhile, cook the broad beans in boiling water to cover for 2–3 minutes, until tender. Drain the beans and cover them with cold water to cool them quickly, then with your fingers pop them out of their grey skins, revealing the brilliant green beans inside.

3. Mix together the dressing ingredients, if using, dress the beans and set aside.

4. Cut the pomegranate in half around its equator. Holding one half over a bowl, cut-side down, bang the surface of the pomegranate with a wooden spoon to release the shiny red seeds; repeat with the other side.

5. Add the broad beans and pomegranate seeds to the cooked quinoa, along with the chopped spring onions and salt to taste.

Warm Salad of Roasted Cauliflower, Watercress and Salty Cheese

Roasted cauliflower is a revelation, with concentrated flavour and lovely crispy bits for added texture. It makes a great warm salad when combined with a salty, crumbly white cheese such as Caerphilly, Wensleydale or Cheshire; read the label or ask at the counter to make sure it's vegetarian.

Serves 4

1 cauliflower, divided into florets, outer leaves removed

125g (4½oz) crumbly white cheese

Bunch of watercress, trimmed

For the lemon and garlic dressing

4 tbsp olive oil

2 garlic cloves, crushed

Juice of 1 lemon

Black pepper

1. Preheat the oven to 200°C (400°F), Gas 6.

2. Slice the cauliflower florets into bite-size pieces. Put into a single layer in a roasting tin or shallow casserole dish. Add the olive oil, garlic, lemon juice and black pepper, and mix so that all the florets get coated.

3. Put into the oven for about 25 minutes, or until the cauliflower is tender and lightly browned in places. Crumble in the cheese, and serve with the watercress.

Quinoa with Basil and Pine Nuts

This is one of my favourite ways to eat the fabulously nutritious grain quinoa. Serve it with a warm Roasted Vegetable Salad (see page 48), for a meal with a sunny Mediterranean flavour.

Serves 2–4

Vegan

200g (7oz) quinoa

400ml (1 pint) water

4 tbsp pine nuts

1 tbsp olive oil

Good bunch of basil, roughly chopped

Salt

1. Put the quinoa into a sieve and wash under the cold tap (see page 48 for why you do this), then put into a saucepan with the water and a pinch of salt, bring to the boil, cover and leave to cook gently for 15 minutes, when the quinoa will be tender and all the water absorbed.

2. Meanwhile, toast the pine nuts by stirring them in a saucepan over a medium heat until they're an even golden brown colour. Immediately tip them on to a plate to prevent them over-browning in the hot pan.

3. Stir the olive oil into the quinoa along with the pine nuts and basil. Serve hot or warm.

Cauliflower Cheese with Mustard, Capers and Cherry Tomatoes

This is such a quick and easy way to make cauliflower cheese, using a smooth cheese instead of making a traditional sauce. You can choose a medium- or low-fat type of cheese but read the ingredients because some of the lighter types contain gelatine (same applies to some yoghurts).

Serves 4

1 cauliflower, trimmed and cut into 1cm (½in) pieces
300g (11oz) cream cheese
1 tsp Dijon mustard
200g (7oz) Cheddar, or Parmesan-style cheese, grated
1–2 tbsp capers, drained and rinsed
250g (9oz) cherry tomatoes, halved
Salt and black pepper
3–4 heaped tbsp breadcrumbs

1. Preheat the grill to high.

2. Cook the cauliflower in 5cm (2in) boiling water for about 8 minutes, or until tender. Drain, and return the cauliflower to the pan.

3. Mix the cream cheese and mustard with the cauliflower, then stir in the two-thirds of the hard cheese, the capers and tomatoes. Season with a little salt if necessary and plenty of pepper.

4. Transfer the mixture into a shallow gratin dish. Scatter the breadcrumbs and remaining cheese on top.

5. Put under the grill for 10–15 minutes, or until the top is golden brown and the inside hot and bubbling. Serve at once – a watercress salad or some quickly cooked green beans go well with this.

Superfood Salad

Raw beetroot is packed with nutrients, boosts the immune system, cleanses the liver and even delivers a natural high through its effect on the body's serotonin. It also tastes good – I love it. I've also added other ingredients renowned for their health-enhancing properties.

Serves 4

100g (3½oz) quinoa

200ml (7fl oz) water

1 raw beetroot

2 tbsp cider vinegar

2 tbsp olive oil or flaxseed oil
(see tip below)

230g (8oz) mixed organic sprouts
(see tip below)

150g (5oz) seed and fruit mix,
containing goji berries, dried
cranberries and blueberries,
sunflower seeds, pumpkin seeds
and pine nuts

1–3 tsp manuka or other thick honey

Sea salt (or pink Himalayan salt if
you're really going over the top
on this!)

Watercress or other green leaves,
to serve

1. Rinse the quinoa in a sieve under the cold tap to remove any possible traces of saponin, a natural bitter coating to the grain: it is usually all removed before packaging; but best to be sure. Then put it into a saucepan with the water, bring to the boil, cover and cook for about 15 minutes, or until all the water has been absorbed and the quinoa is tender and has opened up, with its outer coil.

2. Meanwhile, scrub the beetroot if it's organic, or peel it if not, then grate it into a large bowl. Add the quinoa (which can be still warm), the cider vinegar, olive or flaxseed oil, sprouts and seed and fruit mix. Stir gently; taste, and add honey and salt.

3. I like to serve this with some bright green leaves: watercress is perfect. This salad keeps well, so is a useful one to prepare in advance.

Tips: Flaxseed oil is a wonderful source of omega 3 for vegetarians, but in order to be effective and health-giving, it has to be very fresh, so keep it in the fridge and use within 3–4 weeks. It freezes well, so you could decant some and keep it in the freezer till needed.

You can buy organic beansprouts at health shops and most large supermarkets. They're also very easy to grow yourself at home, if you have the time.

Make it vegan: Use maple syrup instead of honey.

Warm Butternut Squash with Baby-leaf Spinach, Red Onion and Pine Nuts

This is easy to make, and delicious. Though it's so simple, the blend and balance of the flavours, textures and colours – the sharpness of the spinach and the dressing with the dense, sweet and silky butternut squash, the crunch of the red onion and the rich pine nuts – is lovely. It makes a great side dish, or have it with some cooked rice or couscous for a complete meal.

Serves 4

Vegan

1 medium butternut squash

4 tbsp olive oil

50g (2oz) pine nuts

4 tbsp cider vinegar

2 tbsp red wine vinegar

1 red onion, finely chopped

About 6 handfuls (about 50–75g/ 2–3oz) baby spinach leaves

Salt and black pepper

1. Either preheat the oven to 200°C (400°F), Gas 6, or have a large lidded saucepan ready.

2. Peel the butternut squash: this is amazingly easy to do if you use one of those T-shaped swivel-blade potato peelers. Cut the butternut squash into 1cm (½in) cubes, discarding the seeds and stringy bits in the centre.

3. Put the butternut squash into a roasting tin or into your large saucepan if you're using that, and toss with the olive oil. Roast in the oven, or put on a burner, and cook gently until the butternut squash is tender to the point of a knife; in either case, stir it often, and don't let it get brown.

4. While the squash is cooking, toast the pine nuts by stirring them in a dry pan over a gentle heat for a couple of minutes or so until they begin to smell toasty and to brown slightly: tip them out of the pan immediately to prevent overcooking.

5. When the butternut squash is done, put it into a large bowl and gently stir in the cider vinegar, wine vinegar, red onion, spinach leaves (which remain uncooked) and salt and pepper to taste. Scatter with the pine nuts and serve straight away, while the squash is still lovely and warm.

Grilled Aubergine with Halloumi and Mint

A relaxed and easy summer dish that shows just how tender and tasty aubergine can be. You can make it on the grill or the barbecue. Serve with plenty of warm bread to mop up the juices, and a green salad.

Serves 4

2 medium aubergines, cut into
   slices about 6mm (¼in) thick
450g (1lb) halloumi cheese,
   drained and cut into slices slightly
   thicker than the aubergines
2–3 tbsp olive oil
4 tbsp chopped fresh mint

For the balsamic marinade

1 tbsp shoyu soy sauce
1 tbsp maple syrup
2 tbsp balsamic vinegar
3 tbsp olive oil
2 large garlic cloves, crushed
Good pinch of cayenne pepper
Black pepper

1. Make the marinade by mixing all the ingredients together.

2. Put the aubergine slices into a shallow container and cover with the marinade, making sure they're all coated on both sides. If you are cooking them under the grill, you can leave them in this container, if it's heatproof, or you could take them out and cook them on a fine mesh grid over a barbecue.

3. Grill or barbecue the aubergine for about 10 minutes on both sides, until it's beautifully tender.

4. Meanwhile, either brush the halloumi slices with olive oil and cook them on a griddle, for about 3 minutes on each side, or until they have deep brown grid marks; or dry-fry them, without any oil, in a frying pan for 1–2 minutes on each side until lightly browned.

5. Put the grilled aubergine on a large serving platter. If there is any excess marinade, pour this over them, then top with the halloumi, scatter with chopped mint, and serve.

Avocado and Roasted Potato Salad with Creamy Dressing

This is a gorgeous salad of leaves, crunchy chunks of roast potato and buttery avocado, swirled with a creamy dressing and scattered with refreshing dill. It's like eating a hot, rather decadent Caesar salad... I like to use Maris Piper potatoes for this, because you can rely on them to get gloriously golden and crisp.

Serves 4

2 large potatoes, scrubbed and cut into 3cm (1¼in) cubes

8 tbsp olive or rapeseed oil

50g (2oz) semolina

2 large avocados

Juice of 1 lemon

4 tbsp bought mayonnaise

Mixed lettuce leaves, including some red ones

2–4 tbsp roughly chopped fresh dill

Salt and black pepper

1. Preheat the oven to 230ºC (450ºF), Gas 8.

2. Cook the potatoes in 1cm (½in) boiling water for 8 minutes, until almost tender. Just before they're done, pour the oil on to a roasting tin and put into the oven to heat.

3. Drain the potatoes well and scatter with the semolina, turning them so they all get coated.

4. Put the potatoes into the oil (no need to turn them at this point) and bake until golden brown and crisp, turning them after about 10 minutes.

5. While the potatoes are cooking, peel and stone the avocado and cut into 3cm (1¼in) cubes. Toss in 1 tablespoon of the lemon juice, and season with salt.

6. Mix the mayo with the rest of the lemon juice, adding it gradually to make sure you get the degree of sharpness you like.

7. Remove the potatoes from the oven, blot on kitchen paper, then layer up the pretty lettuce leaves, avocado and potato on individual plates, drizzle with the lemon mayonnaise dressing, and scatter with dill. Serve at once.

Make it vegan: This recipe works beautifully using an egg-free mayonnaise; I particularly like the vegan garlic mayonnaise that health shops sell. You could also use the Tofu Mayonnaise on page 26.

Omelettes

One of the fastest hot dishes you can make, and the variations are endless. See opposite for some suggestions.

Serves 1

2 eggs

2 tbsp chopped fresh herbs, such as chervil, chives and parsley (optional)

Salt and black pepper

15g (½oz) butter

1. Break the eggs into a bowl and beat them lightly until just combined. Add the herbs, if using, and season with salt and pepper.

2. Put a 15cm (6in) frying pan over a medium heat. When it is hot, add the butter, turn the heat up and swirl the butter around – don't let it brown.

3. Pour in the eggs, tilting the pan to distribute them evenly, then, using a fork, draw the set edges towards the centre and let the liquid egg run to the edges. Repeat until the omelette is almost set.

4. Tilt the pan over a warmed plate, then fold the edge of the omelette over to the centre, and let it fold over again on to the plate. Serve immediately.

Omelette Toppings

Asparagus
Boil or steam 2–4 trimmed asparagus spears until just tender, then cut them into 2.5cm (1in) lengths. Spoon the asparagus over the omelette when almost set.

Cheese and Herb
Grate 40g (1½oz) grated Cheddar cheese and add half to the beaten eggs. When the omelette is almost set, sprinkle the remaining cheese over the centre.

Fresh Tomato
Use 1 large fresh tomato, skinned and chopped; warm it through in a little butter in a small pan and season. When the omelette is almost set, spoon the tomato over the centre. You could add some slivers of spring onion, or some fresh basil or other herbs, too, if you like. Turn out the omelette and serve dusted with finely grated fresh Parmesan-style cheese.

Pepper
Grill half a red or yellow pepper, or a combination, until charred, then peel off the skin and slice thinly. Spoon over the omelette when almost set.

Mushroom
Wash, dry and slice 50g (2oz) mushrooms – any type, or a mixture – then sauté them in 15g (½oz) butter until they are tender. Season with salt and pepper, and spoon over the omelette when almost set.

Petits Pois and Mint
Cook 50g (2oz) fresh or frozen petits pois in a little boiling water for 2 minutes. Drain, add a knob of butter and 2 teaspoons of chopped fresh mint. Spoon over the omelette when almost set.

Watercress
Fill the cooked omelette, before folding it over, with a handful of fresh watercress for a salad-and-omelette in one.

Nut Pâté with Date and Mint Chutney

This is one of the nicest nut pâté mixtures I know. It's equally good hot or cold, with a cooked vegetable such as green beans or with a salad. The chutney makes a delicious accompaniment, but if you don't have time to prepare it the pâté is equally good without it.

Serves 2

150g (5oz) low-fat garlic and herb
   soft cheese

150g (5oz) roasted cashew nuts

Dash of Tabasco or hot pepper
   sauce (optional)

50g (2oz) dried breadcrumbs
   (optional)

Salt and black pepper

For the chutney

125g (4½oz) dates

1 small onion, chopped

1 tbsp wine vinegar

3 tbsp water

2 tbsp chopped fresh mint

Pinch of cayenne pepper

1. Make the chutney first to allow time for the flavours to develop: chop the dates then put them into a saucepan with the onion, vinegar and water. Cover and cook gently for about 5 minutes, until both have softened and the mixture is no longer liquid.

2. Remove from the heat and add the chopped mint, cayenne pepper and some salt and pepper to taste. Transfer to a bowl and leave on one side.

3. Next make the pâté: put the cheese into a bowl and mash until soft and creamy. Grind the nuts in a food processor or with a rotary hand-grater. Stir the nuts into the cheese to form a mixture that is soft but will hold its shape. Add the Tabasco, if you wish, and season with salt and pepper.

4. Form the pâté into a log shape then coat it all over with the breadcrumbs, if you are using these.

5. Serve the pâté as it is (it can be chilled until needed, in which case it will firm up a bit more), or put it under a moderate grill and grill for about 3 minutes each on the top, bottom and sides, until crisp and brown and heated right through. Cut into 6 slices and serve with the date and mint chutney, if you're having this.

Make it vegan: For a delicious vegan version, use vegan garlic and herb cream cheese, which you can get at health shops and some large supermarkets, instead of dairy cream cheese.

Beautiful Bruschette and Crostini

Bruschette and crostini are essentially the same – crisp slices of bread or baguette with toppings – but bruschette are usually bigger and more rustic, while crostini are more of a dainty 'bite'. The fillings and toppings can be as varied and colourful as you like. I usually spread them first with something to stick the toppings on, then build on top of that with ingredients that can be found in the deli, and end with herbs, chopped or in sprigs; there's plenty to choose from.

Serves 6

For the bases

1 baguette

Olive oil

Salt and black pepper

Smooth goat's cheese (optional)

For the hummus

400g tin chickpeas, drained,
    liquid saved

1 garlic clove, crushed

2 tbsp freshly squeezed lemon juice

1–2 tbsp tahini

A few drops of ume plum seasoning
    (optional; see tip on page 59)

Salt and black pepper

1. Preheat the oven to 150°C (300°F), Gas 2.

2. Slice the bread about 8mm (¼in) thick using a wide baguette for the bruschette or a slim one for the crostini. Brush each slice lightly on both sides with olive oil. Place on a baking sheet and bake for about 20 minutes until crisp. Remove from the oven and transfer to wire racks to cool.

3. Meanwhile make the hummus. Blend the ingredients together with a hand-held blender, or in a freestanding blender, until very smooth and creamy, adding a little of the reserved liquid from the tin to lighten the mixture if necessary. Season with a few drops of ume seasoning, if you have it, and salt as necessary.

4. Spread each crostini/bruschetta with hummus or smooth goat's cheese, then top with pretty and tasty ingredients.

A few suggestions for the toppings

Hummus or goat's cheese with marinated barbecued artichokes and shavings of Parmesan-style cheese.

Hummus or goat's cheese with roasted red and gold peppers from the deli.

Hummus or goat's cheese with black olives and chopped coriander leaves.

Soft goat's cheese with pomegranate seeds and chopped coriander leaves.

Soft goat's cheese with cooked beetroot, diced and mixed with thick yoghurt and chopped spring onions.

Tandoori Potato Skewers with Minty Raita

Surprising though it may seem, one of the best vegetables to cook on a skewer is potatoes. They're especially good if you coat them with a spicy paste before grilling. Serve them with minty raita and warm naan bread. You'll need four skewers for this recipe.

Serves 4

24 baby new potatoes, scrubbed

For the tandoori paste

2 garlic cloves, crushed

2 tbsp ground cumin

2 tbsp olive oil

Juice of ½ lemon

Salt and black pepper

For the minty raita

300ml (11fl oz) plain natural yoghurt

4 tbsp chopped mint

1. Boil the potatoes in water to cover until you can just get the point of a knife or skewer into them: about 5–10 minutes, depending on their size. Drain and cool quickly by rinsing under the cold tap.

2. While the potatoes are cooking, make the paste: simply mix all the ingredients together.

3. Thread the potatoes on to the skewers, then use your fingers to coat them all over with the paste.

4. Grill for 15–20 minutes, until the potatoes are crisp and brown, turning the skewers from time to time so they cook evenly.

5. To make the minty raita, combine the yoghurt with the chopped mint and a little salt. Put into a small serving bowl or jug.

Make it vegan: Use soya yoghurt in place of dairy yoghurt.

Onion Bhajees

These are lovely served as a starter, but they also make a filling meal served with some plainly cooked rice, chutney and perhaps a raita (see opposite).

Serves 2–4

Vegan

125g (4½oz) chickpea (gram) flour

2 tsp ground coriander

1 tsp ground cumin

Pinch of cayenne pepper

1 tsp salt

150ml (5fl oz) tepid water

Rapeseed oil, for deep-frying

1 onion, finely chopped

1 tbsp chopped fresh coriander (optional)

1. Preheat the oven to 150°C (300°F) Gas 2. Sift the chickpea flour into a bowl with the ground coriander, cumin and cayenne. Add the salt, then pour in the tepid water and stir to make a batter.

2. Heat some oil in a deep-fryer or large saucepan. Stir the chopped onion, and the fresh coriander if you are using this, into the batter, then, when the oil is hot, drop teaspoonfuls of the mixture into the pan and fry, in batches, for about 5 minutes, until they are really crisp and the onion is cooked through. Turn them so they brown evenly.

3. Drain the bhajees on kitchen paper and eat straight away while they're hot and crisp.

Vietnamese Spring Rolls with Balsamic Reduction

These are really pretty and easy to make. You can get rice paper wrappers in Asian shops or large supermarkets; you can get larger ones, about 22cm diameter, or smaller ones, about 16cm. The filling here is enough for 1 packet of the larger ones, or 2 packets of smaller ones. I prefer working with the larger ones because they're quicker and less fiddly, but the smaller ones are nice for a party.

Makes about 10–12 large spring rolls or 18–20 small ones
Vegan

200g (7oz) grated carrot
200g (7oz) beansprouts
1 tbsp chopped fresh mint
1 tbsp chopped flat-leaf parsley
2 tbsp mirin
2 tbsp olive oil
2 tbsp rice or cider vinegar
Salt
6 small spring onions, cut into thin strips
1 red pepper, cut into thin strips
1 medium avocado, peeled, stoned and cut into thin strips
2 × 50g packets small rice flour pancakes, or 134g packet large rice flour pancakes

For the balsamic reduction

8 tbsp balsamic vinegar – adequate quality, not an expensive one
2 tbsp maple syrup

1. Start by making the balsamic reduction: it can be simmering on the stove while you make the spring rolls. Just put the balsamic vinegar into a non-metal pan and let it bubble on the burner until it has reduced by half. Remove from the heat and stir in the maple syrup. Cool.

2. To make the filling for the spring rolls, mix the grated carrot, beansprouts, chopped mint and parsley, mirin, olive oil and rice or cider vinegar. Season with salt. Lay out the strips of spring onion, red pepper and avocado.

3. Spread a clean damp tea towel over your work surface. Put the rice pancakes into a bowl, cover with hot water and leave to soak for about 20 seconds, or until they become flexible. Remove them from the water and spread them out on the tea towel.

4. Take about 2 tablespoons of the carrot mixture and place on one of the pancakes towards the edge nearest to you, and put some spring onion, a piece of red pepper, and a piece of avocado on top. Fold the two sides of the wrapper in, then the bottom edge so that it covers the filling. Roll this over again, holding in the filling, and keep rolling until you have a firmly packed spring roll. Put this on a plate, seam-side down.

5. Continue in this way until all the pancakes are used. Cover the finished rolls with the clean damp tea towel until required. Serve with the balsamic reduction in a small bowl.

Tip: You could serve the spring rolls with a red chilli dipping sauce or hoisin sauce instead; both are available at supermarkets.

Tempura Vegetables

Everybody loves crisp, golden-battered vegetables straight out of the pan. They're lovely as a snack for a special treat and, surprising though it may seem, I love tempura for a party, too (see the tip below).

Serves 4

Vegan

Rapeseed oil, for deep-frying

500g (1lb 2oz) vegetables:
   100g (3½oz) each of five of the following: broccoli florets (these make particularly delicious tempura), wedges of red onion, pieces of red pepper, 6mm (¼in) slices from a slim sweet potato, chunky slices of courgette, asparagus spears, baby sweetcorn

For the batter

100g (3½oz) plain white flour

200g (7oz) cornflour

½ tsp salt

3 tsp baking powder

About 400ml (14fl oz) sparkling water

1. Half-fill one or two woks, deep-frying pans or large heavy saucepans with rapeseed oil. Heat until a small cube of bread sizzles and rises to the surface immediately and browns in 1 minute.

2. While the oil is heating, mix the batter. Put the flours, salt and baking powder into a bowl, add the sparkling water and mix quickly, using a fork or chopstick: it needs to remain a bit lumpy and some bits of flour don't matter. You need a consistency that will coat the vegetables lightly – do a test one and see how it is; add a bit more water or cornflour to adjust as necessary.

3. Dip a selection of about 5 vegetables in the batter and fry for about 2 minutes, until golden and crisp. Lift out with a slotted spoon or kitchen tongs, blot lightly with kitchen paper then serve, or, as this batter stays pretty crisp, you can keep them in a warm oven for a few minutes while you make more.

4. Immediately coat more vegetables with batter and fry; keep repeating the process for as long as it takes!

5. If you like you can serve the Tempura Vegetables with a dip. Choose from the Soured Cream Dip (opposite), the Caper Sauce (page 33), Tofu Mayonnaise (page 26), or any of the Trio of Dips (page 29). Sweet chilli sauce also makes a great dip for tempura.

Tip: Frying tempura for a crowd is surprisingly easy. The secret is to have everything ready and laid out beforehand and a kind helper to serve the tempura as it comes out of the pan.

Rösti Potato 'Crisps' with Soured Cream and Chive Dip

These crisp, golden mini röstis are quick to do and irresistible! They look like big ridged crisps, hence the name, and are delectable to munch just on their own, or with a creamy dip as suggested, or even tomato ketchup. If you want to make a bit more of a light meal of it, try adding a salad of diced cooked beetroot tossed in cider vinegar or brown rice vinegar, and some watercress.

Serves 2–4

500g (1lb 2oz) organic baking potatoes, scrubbed

Rapeseed oil, for shallow-frying

For the soured cream dip

1 tbsp chopped chives

150ml (5fl oz) soured cream

Salt and pepper

1. Grate the potatoes coarsely: this doesn't take long using a box grater. Wrap the grated potato in a cloth and squeeze as much liquid out of it as you can.

2. Cover the base of a frying pan lightly with rapeseed oil and heat. Put in small handfuls of the grated potato mixture and press them down with a spatula, to make flat rösti about 7.5cm (3in) in diameter. Fry them until crisp and golden – about 2 minutes – then flip them over using the spatula and fry the other side until it is crisp and golden brown too: 1–2 minutes. Drain the rösti on kitchen paper.

3. Repeat until all the potato has been used and you have about 16 rösti crisps.

4. While the rösti are cooking, make the dip: mix the chives into the soured cream and season. Serve with the rösti. The rösti are nice sprinkled with salt too.

Make it vegan: Use vegan cream for the dip.

Spanakopita with Tzatziki

These crisp golden filo pastries filled with spinach and feta are very easy to make, and instant nostalgia for anyone who loves holidaying in Greece. This recipe makes enough pastries for a party: about 30, using a whole packet of filo. If you want to make fewer, just halve the ingredients; if you wrap the remaining filo carefully it will keep in the freezer.

Makes 30

500g (1lb 2oz) frozen chopped
    spinach, thawed
4 spring onions, finely chopped
200g (7oz) feta cheese, crumbled
Salt and black pepper
1 packet filo pastry
5–6 tbsp olive oil, for brushing

For the tzatziki

½ cucumber, grated, sprinkled
    with salt and drained in a sieve
300ml (11fl oz) thick strained
    Greek yoghurt
1 garlic clove, crushed
1-2 tbsp chopped mint
1–2 tbsp extra virgin olive oil,
    to serve
Fresh mint, to garnish (optional)

1. Preheat the oven to 200°C (400°F), Gas 6.

2. Put the spinach in a sieve or colander and press to remove any excess liquid. Transfer to a bowl and add the spring onions, crumbled feta and salt and pepper to taste.

3. Cut the sheets of filo pastry into strips about 8 × 28cm (3 × 11in); with the type of filo I used, this meant getting 6 strips per sheet, but the measurements don't have to be exactly the same. Keep the strips wrapped in a clean damp tea towel while you work so that they remain pliable.

4. Take one strip, put it in front of you with the short edges at the top and bottom. Brush the surface with olive oil, then put a good heaped teaspoonful of the filling at the top of the pastry strip. Fold one top corner diagonally across to cover the filling and make a triangle. Then fold this triangle over on to the filo, and keep folding over and over until you end up with a plump, triangular parcel. Place this on a baking sheet and brush with a little more oil if necessary.

5. Continue like this until you've used all the filo and filling, and have about 30 spanakopita on the baking sheet. Bake in the oven for about 15 minutes, until golden brown and crisp.

6. Make the tzatziki while the spanakopita are cooking; drain the cucumber and pat it dry on kitchen paper, then mix it with the yoghurt, garlic and mint and season as necessary. Put it into a small bowl and swirl the olive oil over the top and mint to garnish.

7. Serve the spanakopita straight away, with a bowl of tzatziki for dipping.

Everyday Suppers

Potato and Leek Gratin

This is a real winter comfort, delicious just as it is or with a side of winter greens such as kale or Brussels sprouts.

Serves 6

1.5kg (3lb 4oz) potatoes, peeled and cut into 8mm (¼in) slices

400g (14oz) leeks, trimmed and cut into 1cm (½in) slices

Olive oil, for brushing

2 tbsp chopped flat-leaf parsley

200g (7oz) Parmesan-style cheese, grated

8 tbsp double cream or single soya cream

Salt and black pepper

1. Boil the potatoes in water until just tender: about 10 minutes. Drain.

2. In another pan, boil the leeks until tender: about 7 minutes. Drain.

3. Season the potatoes and leeks with salt and pepper.

4. Brush a 23cm (9in) springform tin – or casserole or gratin dish if you prefer – with olive oil. Put a layer of potatoes into the base, then put the leeks on top, scatter with the parsley and half the cheese, and drizzle over the cream. Season with salt and pepper, then top with the rest of the potatoes and grated cheese.

5. Put under a hot grill for 7–10 minutes, or until browned and bubbling round the edges.

Roasted Winter Vegetables with Spiced Lentils and Feta

Such an easy and satisfying meal, and you can change the vegetables as you like, or have beans or chickpeas instead of lentils.

Serves 4

1 leek, cut into 2cm (¾in) pieces

1 red onion, cut into sixths

1 parsnip, peeled and cut into 1cm (½in) cubes

1 large carrot, peeled and cut into 1cm (½in) slices

1 small butternut squash, peeled and cut into 1cm (½in) chunks

1 beetroot, peeled and cut into 1cm (½in) cubes

1 large stick of celery, cut into 2cm (¾in) lengths

¼ cauliflower, in florets

2 tbsp olive oil

Flat-leaf parsley, chopped, and fresh thyme leaves, to serve

200g (7oz) feta cheese, crumbled, to serve

For the lentils

1 tsp ground cumin

1 tsp ground coriander

400g tin Puy or green lentils, drained

1. Preheat the oven to 220°C (425°F), Gas 7.

2. Put all the vegetables into a roasting tin in a single layer and drizzle with the oil. Turn the vegetables gently so that they are all coated. Roast for 20–25 minutes, until the vegetables are tender, turning them after about 15 minutes.

3. When the vegetables are almost done, prepare the spiced lentils: put the cumin and coriander into a saucepan and stir over the heat for a few seconds until they smell aromatic, then immediately stir in the lentils and heat through.

4. Serve the vegetables on a large warm platter, scattered with parsley and thyme, with the lentils and cheese, which could be in separate bowls or mixed lightly with the vegetables.

Broad Bean Lasagne

This is so simple, with just a few ingredients, but it looks and tastes so good. You could use fresh egg lasagne for this, but I prefer to use dried. It looks very pretty made up as individual portions, stacking them up on a baking sheet that will go under the grill, but it tastes just as good made in a big homely dish. Serve it with a crunchy summer lettuce salad with fresh mint in it for lovely complementary flavours and textures.

Serves 4

750g packet of frozen broad beans, thawed

6 sheets of lasagne

250g (9oz) soft white goat's cheese

120ml (4½fl oz) pouring cream

60g Parmesan-style cheese, finely grated

Salt and black pepper

1. Bring a large pan of water to the boil and cook the broad beans briefly, for about 2 minutes.

2. Tip the beans into a colander but save the boiling water, return it to the pan, bring it back to the boil and put the lasagne in; let it cook until tender, following the packet directions.

3. Rinse the broad beans under the cold tap, then pop off, and discard, the outer grey skins.

4. Beat the goat's cheese with a wooden spoon adding about 4 tablespoons of cold water if necessary to make it creamy, then stir in the broad beans. Season well.

5. When the lasagne is cooked, drain it and keep it in cold water until you're ready to assemble the lasagne.

6. Cut the sheets of lasagne in half, so they are roughly square. Take a grill pan or roasting tin that will fit under your grill, line it with a piece of cooking parchment to make sure the lasagne sheets don't stick, then arrange 4 of the pasta squares on top.

7. Spoon some of the broad bean mixture on to each of the squares of lasagne, then put another square on top, followed by more broad bean mixture, then a final square of lasagne, making 4 individual lasagnes in all. Pour 2 tablespoons of cream over the top and scatter with the grated Parmesan-style cheese.

8. Put them under a hot grill or in a hot oven – 220ºC (425ºF) Gas 7 – for about 5 minutes or until heated through and golden brown on top.

Make it vegan: Use lasagne without egg, vegan cream cheese, Alpro soya cream and vegan Parmesan or a few garlic breadcrumbs to sprinkle on top.

Wholemeal Penne with Broccoli and Pesto

Fast, simple, delicious and healthy, a dish that appeals to all ages.

Serves 4

400g (14oz) wholemeal penne

400g (14oz) broccoli (calabrese type)

4 tbsp pesto (see cook's notes on page 8)

Salt and black pepper

A few torn basil leaves, to serve (optional)

1. Bring a large pan of water to the boil and put in the penne. Cook, uncovered, following the packet directions, until al dente.

2. Meanwhile, divide the broccoli into florets, cutting them as necessary to make even bite-size pieces. Five minutes before the penne is done, cook the broccoli in 1cm (½in) boiling water for 4–5 minutes, or until just tender. Drain.

3. Drain the pasta into a colander, then put back into the still-warm pan with the broccoli. Stir in about 4 tablespoons of pesto, or to taste, mixing gently but thoroughly.

4. Season to taste with salt and black pepper, then serve on warmed plates and garnish with a few torn basil leaves, if available.

Make it vegan: Use vegan pesto: there is one made by Zest, which you can get from GoodnessDirect.com or other good wholefood shops.

Quick Mediterranean Pasta

This makes a lovely quick and easy supper, especially if you serve it with a glass of red wine and some garlic bread or a tossed green salad on the side.

Serves 4

2 tbsp olive oil

1 onion, chopped

2 red peppers, deseeded and chopped

1 aubergine, cut into 1cm (½in) dice

2 garlic cloves, crushed

400g tin tomatoes

Handful of black olives – I like Kalamata; jars of pitted ones are good

350g (12oz) penne rigate or rigatoni

Salt and black pepper

Several sprigs of fresh basil leaves, to serve

Flakes of Parmesan-style cheese, to serve (optional)

1. Fill a large saucepan with plenty of water to cook the pasta and bring to the boil. Add the pasta and cook according to the packet directions, until it is al dente.

2. Meanwhile, heat 1 tablespoon of the oil in a saucepan and put in the onion, red peppers and aubergine. Stir, then cover and cook gently for 10 minutes, until the vegetables are becoming tender but not brown.

3. Stir in the garlic, cook for a few seconds, then add the tomatoes, together with their juice, breaking them up with a wooden spoon. Simmer for about 10–15 minutes, until the liquid has evaporated. Stir in the olives, and season with salt and pepper.

4. Drain the pasta, return it to the pan and add the remaining tablespoon of olive oil. Season with some salt; then add the sauce and the basil leaves, and stir so that all the pasta gets coated; or, if you prefer, serve out the pasta and spoon the sauce on top: I know that's not authentically Italian, but some people prefer it. Serve the cheese alongside, if using.

Spaghetti alla Puttanesca

A dish that is full of flavour and interest, and quick to make from store-cupboard ingredients.

Serves 4

Vegan

350g (12oz) spaghetti

2 tbsp olive oil

1 red onion, finely chopped

4 garlic cloves, finely sliced

400g tin cherry tomatoes

4 tbsp small black olives such as Niçois, or Kalamata would be fine too

4 tbsp small salted capers: I prefer the type preserved in vinegar, such as capers surfines, drained

1 tsp dried oregano

Dried chilli flakes, to taste

Salt and black pepper

2 tbsp flat-leaf parsley leaves, to serve

1. Bring a pan of water to the boil for the pasta; add the spaghetti and cook according to the packet directions until al dente.

2. Meanwhile, heat 1 tablespoon of the olive oil in another saucepan, put in the onion and cook gently for 5 minutes, then add the garlic, cherry tomatoes, along with their liquid, the olives, capers and oregano. Let the mixture cook over a medium heat for 5 minutes, stirring often. Add salt, pepper and chilli flakes to taste.

3. Drain the pasta and return it to the saucepan with the remaining tbsp of olive oil; mix gently until it is all glossy, and season with some salt.

4. Add the sauce to the pasta in the pan, gently moving the pasta around to distribute the sauce. Check the seasoning, adding more salt if necessary and another grinding of black pepper. Serve on to warm plates, and top with some torn parsley leaves.

Spaghetti with Lentil Bolognaise

This is the recipe that saw one of my daughters and her friends through medical school, and it's still a family favourite. Originally I used dried lentils to make it, but although dried Puy lentils soften quickly, you can't get them quite tender enough to bring them into the 30-minute category – but tinned Puy lentils are now widely available, and taste great.

Serves 4

3 tbsp olive oil

2 onions, finely chopped

2 carrots, finely chopped

2 celery sticks, finely chopped

4–5 garlic cloves, crushed

1 tsp dried oregano

2 × 400g tins Puy lentils, drained,
 liquid reserved

400g tin chopped tomatoes

2 tbsp tomato purée

Salt and black pepper

350g (12oz) spaghetti

Grated Parmesan-style cheese,
 to serve (optional)

1. Heat 2 tablespoons of the olive oil in a large saucepan, add the onions and cook for 5 minutes, letting them brown a bit. Then stir in the carrots, celery, garlic and oregano. Cook gently, covered, for 15 minutes, or until tender, stirring from time to time.

2. Add the lentils, tomatoes and tomato purée to the onion mixture, and enough of the reserved lentil liquid to make a thick, soft consistency. Season with salt and black pepper, then leave to cook over a gentle heat.

3. Meanwhile, bring another large saucepan of water to the boil and cook the spaghetti according to the packet directions. Drain and return to the still-hot saucepan, and toss in the remaining tablespoon of olive oil and seasoning to taste.

4. Add the bolognaise to the spaghetti, mix gently and serve; or spoon the sauce on top of the spaghetti if you prefer it this way. Serve with the grated cheese, if you are having this.

Macaroni Cheese

I've never known a child not to like macaroni cheese – as long as I keep it simple and classic, that is. If you're cooking for more adventurous palates, the dish can be varied in all kinds of ways: try adding cherry tomatoes, mushrooms, chopped onion, or perk it up by increasing the amount of mustard and adding capers. If there's any over, try making it into croquettes, coating with breadcrumbs and shallow-frying (see page 33 for my recommended coating for a crisp result).

Serves 4

175g (6oz) quick-cooking macaroni

50g (2oz) butter, in pieces

50g (2oz) plain flour

500ml (18fl oz) milk (see tip below)

1 tsp Dijon mustard

100g (3½oz) finely grated
Parmesan-style or similar cheese

Salt and black pepper

For the topping

2 handfuls soft breadcrumbs

2–3 tbsp finely grated
Parmesan-style cheese

1. Bring a large saucepan of water to the boil and cook the macaroni, without a lid on the pan, for about 8 minutes or until al dente.

2. Meanwhile, make the cheese sauce: put the butter, flour, milk and mustard into a saucepan and bring to the boil, whisking, until thick and smooth.

3. Let the sauce simmer gently for a few minutes to cook the flour. Remove from the heat and stir in the cheese.

4. Heat the grill. When the macaroni is done, drain and add to the sauce, and season with salt and pepper.

5. Put the macaroni cheese into a shallow heatproof dish and top with a light scattering of breadcrumbs and the cheese. Grill for a few minutes until the topping is golden brown.

Tip: Use whatever type of milk you like. My choice would be unsweetened rice or oat milk, from health shops and many supermarkets, or soya milk, also unsweetened.

Fried Rice with Cashew Nuts and Asparagus

An excellent way of saving time is to think ahead and use 'planned leftovers'; rice is particularly good for this. Here it is lightly fried with a selection of vegetables and finished off with roasted cashew nuts and asparagus – but you could use other vegetables, or toasted pine nuts or pumpkin seeds instead of cashews.

Serves 4

Vegan

2 onions, sliced

2 tbsp toasted sesame oil

½ pointed pale green cabbage, sliced, tough centre removed

500g (1lb 2oz) cooked rice (see tip below)

125g (4½oz) frozen petits pois, thawed

1 bunch asparagus, tough ends broken off

1–2 tbsp shoyu soy sauce

1–2 tsp ume seasoning, if available (see tip below)

Salt and black pepper

100g (3½oz) roasted cashew nuts, to serve

Chopped flat-leaf parsley or coriander, to serve (optional)

1. In a large, deep frying pan, or saucepan, fry the onions in the oil for about 5 minutes, until beginning to soften, stirring often. Then put in the cabbage and continue to cook gently for another 5 minutes or so, until tender.

2. Add the cooked rice and the peas to the frying pan, and stir-fry over a moderate heat for a few minutes until everything is heated through.

3. Meanwhile, cook the asparagus in 1cm (½in) boiling water, with a lid on the pan, for about 7 minutes, or until it is tender when tested with the point of a knife, then drain and keep it warm.

4. Season the rice mixture with shoyu, ume seasoning if you're using it, and salt and pepper.

5. Serve the rice out on to warmed plates, top with asparagus spears, roasted cashew nuts, and chopped herbs if you have them.

Tips: Brown basmati rice is excellent, as are the basmati and wild rice mixes you can buy in many supermarkets. I'm also particularly fond of organic short-grain brown rice, but it takes 45 minutes to cook.

You can buy ume seasoning at large wholefood shops and some supermarkets. I love it because just a few drops really bring out the flavour of food. It's very salty; you only need a teaspoonful or so.

Celery Rice with Toasted Almonds and Watercress and Carrot Sauté

There's something almost zen-like about eating this; it makes me feel balanced, calmed and relaxed. The flavours are natural and gentle, which is part of its charm, so you're very aware of the nuttiness of the brown rice, the saltiness of the celery, the intense sweetness of the carrots. If you'd like your flavours a bit more intense, though, feel free to rev them up with some soy sauce or a sprinkling of chilli. I've used brown basmati rice here because it will cook in 30 minutes, but if you've a bit longer to spare, it's worth trying it with organic short-grain brown rice; you cook it in the same way but it takes 40–45 minutes.

Serves 4

Vegan

For the celery rice

6 celery sticks, any tough strands shaved off with a swivel-blade peeler, diced

200g (7oz) brown basmati rice, rinsed

500ml (18fl oz) water

50g (2oz) flaked almonds

For the carrot and watercress sauté

1 tbsp toasted sesame oil

500g (1lb 2oz) carrots, cut in very slim slices, straight or on the slant

8 spring onions, sliced on the diagonal

1 bunch or packet of watercress, trimmed

A few drops of shoyu soy sauce

1. Put the celery into a pan with the rice and water. Bring to the boil, then cover, reduce the heat, and leave to cook gently for 25 minutes, or until the rice is tender and all the water has been absorbed.

2. Meanwhile, toast the almonds by stirring them in a dry pan over a moderate heat for 2–3 minutes, until they turn golden brown and smell toasted. Remove from the pan immediately.

3. Heat the sesame oil in another pan, add the carrots and give them a stir, then turn the heat down low, cover the pan and leave to cook very gently. Look at the carrots after 4–5 minutes, give the pan a shake and add a splash of water if they are showing signs of sticking. Cover and cook for about 5 more minutes, or until the carrots are tender.

4. Add the spring onions to the carrots, stir, and cook for 1–2 minutes, then add the watercress and stir-fry for 1 minute, just to wilt it slightly. Season with a few drops of shoyu soy sauce.

5. Serve the rice scattered with the almonds, the carrot sauté beside it.

Egyptian Rice and Lentils with Caramelised Onions and Pine Nuts

This is easy to make, nourishing and tasty. It's delicious served with some steamed spinach.

Serves 4

Vegan

200g (7oz) brown basmati rice, rinsed
500ml (18fl oz) water
4 onions, sliced into thin rings
2 tbsp olive oil
4 garlic cloves, crushed
4 tsp ground cumin
4 tsp ground coriander
2 × 400g tins Puy or green lentils, drained
Salt and pepper
50g (2oz) pine nuts, toasted, to serve
4 tbsp chopped flat-leaf parsley, to serve

1. Put the rice into a pan with the water, bring to the boil, then cover and leave to cook very gently for 25 minutes, until the rice is tender and the water absorbed.

2. Meanwhile, fry the onions gently in the oil until they are golden brown and slightly caramelised: about 20 minutes. Remove half the onions from the pan and set aside, keeping them warm.

3. Add the garlic, cumin and coriander to the remaining onions in the pan, along with the drained lentils, and cook over a low heat, stirring from time to time.

4. Stir the cooked rice gently with a fork, then add this to the pan with the onions and spices, and stir until everything is mixed. Season with salt and pepper.

5. Serve the rice and lentils on one large or 4 individual warm plates; pile the reserved onions on top and scatter with toasted pine nuts and chopped parsley.

Oven-baked Asparagus and Pea Risotto

Let the oven do the work for you on a sunny early summer day when you'd rather be outside than standing over the stove, stirring! I love this as a main course with a very fresh salad of tender leaves.

Serves 4

900ml (1½ pints) boiling water

1 tsp vegetable stock powder

1 onion, chopped

2 celery sticks, finely chopped

1 tbsp olive oil

2 garlic cloves, chopped

350g (12oz) risotto rice

100ml (3½fl oz) white wine, sherry, Noilly Prat or dry Martini

350g (12oz) asparagus spears, trimmed and halved

200g (7oz) frozen petits pois, thawed

Salt and black pepper

Chopped mint, to serve

Flaked or finely grated Parmesan-style cheese, to serve (optional)

1. Preheat the oven to 200ºC (400ºF), Gas 6. Place a large casserole dish (or a roasting tin), for cooking the risotto, in to the oven to heat. Put the boiling water into a saucepan with the stock powder, stir, and keep hot over a gentle heat.

2. Fry the onion and celery in the olive oil in a large saucepan for 5 minutes, until beginning to soften, then add the garlic and the rice. Stir for 1–2 minutes over the heat, then add the wine, sherry or dry martini, 1 teaspoon salt, a grinding of black pepper, and let it bubble over the heat until the liquid has been absorbed.

3. Put the rice mixture into your heated casserole, then pour in the boiling stock. Stir quickly to distribute all the ingredients evenly, then bake, uncovered, for 20 minutes or until the rice is tender but still holding its shape and the stock has been absorbed.

4. When the risotto has 10 minutes before it is ready, cook the asparagus in a little boiling water for 4–6 minutes, or until just tender; add the peas to the pan to heat them through, then drain.

5. Once the risotto is done, stir very well to bring out the creaminess, check the seasoning, add the asparagus, peas and chopped mint, fork through, and serve immediately, with Parmesan-style cheese, if you like.

Tip: Any leftovers make the most beautiful croquettes. Form the cold mixture into balls, dip in flour then beaten egg, or in a mixture of cornflour and water (see page 33), then in dry breadcrumbs, and deep-fry until crisp. Lovely with a horseradish or a tomato sauce.

Borlotti Bean and Mushroom Stew

This is easy to make, warming and satisfying; great for a chilly day. Try it with some Millet, Cauliflower and Parsley Mash (see page 189), for a perfectly balanced meal of bean, grain and greens; or achieve this more simply with warm bread and a quickly cooked green vegetable such as kale. There's time to make the mash while the stew cooks.

Serves 4

Vegan

1 tbsp olive oil

1 onion, chopped

2 large carrots, sliced into rings

2 large leeks, sliced into rings

5 outer celery sticks, sliced

300g (11oz) button mushrooms

2 garlic cloves, crushed

2 sprigs of thyme

2 × 400g tins borlotti beans, drained and rinsed

1½ tbsp plain flour

100ml (3½fl oz) red wine

600ml (1 pint) water

2 tsp vegetable stock powder

2 tbsp shoyu soy sauce

Salt and black pepper

Chopped flat-leaf parsley, to serve

1. Heat the oil in a large pan, add the onion, carrots, leeks and celery, and fry for 5 minutes, stirring to prevent sticking.

2. Add the mushrooms, garlic, thyme and beans, then stir in the flour and cook for 2 minutes.

3. Pour in the wine and water and stir in the stock powder, soy sauce and seasoning. Bring to the boil. Simmer gently for 20 minutes until all the vegetables are tender. Serve sprinkled with chopped parsley.

Red Bean Wraps

Of course you could use bought wraps for these, but I prefer to make my own, and once you find out how easy they are to do and how good they taste, I think you will, too. You can fill them with any mixture of beans, salad, cooked rice or vegetables you like. I love this mixture of red beans, lettuce, tomato and avocado.

Makes 6

For the wraps

150g (5oz) spelt flour

¼ tsp salt

2 tbsp olive oil

About 4 tbsp water

A little olive oil for frying

For the filling

4 handfuls of mixed leafy salad

400g tin red kidney beans,
    drained and mashed

4 tomatoes, chopped

1 avocado, peeled, stoned and sliced

Small bunch fresh coriander,
    chopped

Salt and black pepper

Soured cream, to serve (optional)

1. Make the wraps: put the spelt flour into a bowl. Add the salt and oil, and enough water to make a soft dough – the consistency of soft modelling clay. Divide the dough into 6 even-sized pieces. Roll each piece into a ball and flatten it with the palm of your hand, then roll out into a thin round, about 15cm (6in) across.

2. Heat a little oil, about 1 tablespoonful, in a frying pan. Add one of the circles of dough and fry until set and flecked with brown on one side, then flip it over and fry the other side. Remove the wrap from the frying pan and fry the rest in the same way. Add a little more oil if necessary, but the wraps don't need much oil; the pan really only needs to be 'oiled'. Pile them up on a plate as they're done.

3. Spread out one of the wraps on a board, put some lettuce, mashed beans, tomatoes, avocado and coriander on top, season with salt and pepper, fold the two sides of the wrap in over the filling, then fold up the bottom edge and roll up tightly. Repeat with the rest of the wraps and filling. Serve with soured cream, if you're using this.

Make it vegan: Leave the soured cream out or replace it with a vegan version.

Lentil Chilli Croquettes with Dill Sauce

These lentil croquettes are crunchy on the outside, tender within, and the hot chilli contrasts with the cooling yoghurt and dill sauce. They're crispest if they're deep-fried, but shallow-frying works well too (see tip below).

Serves 4

1 onion, chopped

1 tbsp olive oil

2 garlic cloves, crushed

1 fresh green chilli, deseeded and
    chopped, or chilli powder to taste

4 tsp ground coriander

2 × 400g tins green lentils, drained

Rapeseed oil, for frying
    (see tip below)

2 slices of bread, crusts removed

Small bunch of coriander, chopped

Salt and black pepper

For the coating

120g (4oz) cornflour

½ tsp salt

90–120ml (3½–4½fl oz) water

100g (3½oz) fine dried breadcrumbs

For the dill sauce

3 tbsp chopped fresh dill

300ml (11fl oz) creamy yoghurt
    or soured cream

1. Fry the onion in the oil, with a lid on the pan, for 5 minutes. Add the garlic, chilli and ground coriander, then cover and cook for 2–3 minutes. Remove from the heat and stir in the lentils.

2. If you are going to deep-fry the burgers, put the oil on to heat, but keep your eye on it. Cover the bread with water, drain immediately, then squeeze out all the water and crumble the bread – this is a quick way of making breadcrumbs. Add to the lentil mixture along with the fresh coriander and seasoning, mashing the mixture with the spoon or a potato masher so that it holds together.

3. Divide the mixture into eight and form into balls if you are going to deep-fry them, or flattish burger shapes for shallow-frying.

4. To make the coating, mix the cornflour and salt with enough water to make a mixture that is soft enough to dip the croquettes into but stiff enough to stick to them; I mix with my fingers as I gradually add the water, so that I can feel when it reaches this stage.

5. Dip the croquettes first in the cornflour mixture, then into the crumbs, to coat them all over. Gently drop the croquettes in the oil and fry for about 3–4 minutes on each side if shallow-frying and 4–5 minutes in total if deep-frying. Drain them well on kitchen paper.

6. Serve with a sauce made by stirring the chopped dill into the creamy yoghurt or soured cream and seasoning with salt and pepper.

Tip: When deep-frying small quantities of food, you can do it quickly using a medium saucepan rather than a deep-fryer. This means you also use a lot less oil, which makes it feasible to use good-quality cold-pressed rapeseed oil.

Ultimate Red Bean Chilli

This makes a big, colourful chilli; serve it with some couscous, baby new potatoes or crusty bread and maybe some chopped avocado or Guacamole (see page 29) on the side; you could go to town and throw in bowls of olives, tortilla chips and grated cheese for an easy, fun, crowd-pleasing supper.

Serves 4

2 tbsp olive oil

2 onions, chopped

1 large red pepper,
    deseeded and chopped

1 yellow pepper,
    deseeded and chopped

1 green pepper,
    deseeded and chopped

2–4 garlic cloves, finely chopped

1 mild red chilli, deseeded and
    finely chopped

2 tsp ground coriander

2 × 400g tins green lentils, drained

2 × 400g tins red kidney beans,
    drained

2 × 400g tins chopped tomatoes

Chilli powder (optional)

Salt and black pepper

Soured cream, to serve

Chopped flat-leaf parsley
    or coriander, to serve

1. Heat the oil in a medium-large saucepan, then add the onion and peppers, cover and cook for 15–20 minutes, or until the vegetables are tender. Stir them from time to time to prevent them sticking to the pan.

2. Add the garlic, chopped chilli, coriander, lentils, red kidney beans and tomatoes and cook, uncovered, for 5–10 minutes, until everything is heated through.

3. Add some chilli powder to taste, if necessary; season with salt and pepper. Serve with a swirl of soured cream and some chopped parsley or coriander.

Make it vegan: Use vegan soured cream.

Courgette Balls in a Spicy Sauce

This is my much simplified and speeded-up version of a Madhur Jaffrey recipe –
even so, it does take the full 30 minutes, but the result is worth it. It's lovely with
plain white basmati rice.

Serves 4

Vegan

2 medium onions,
    very finely chopped

1 tbsp olive oil

¼ tsp turmeric

1 tsp ground cumin

2 tsp ground coriander

250g (9oz) tomatoes,
    peeled and chopped

400ml tin coconut milk –
    use half, the rest freezes
    well for another time

For the balls

500g (1lb 2oz) courgettes,
    coarsely grated

1 tsp grated fresh ginger

2 tbsp chopped coriander

50g (2oz) chickpea flour

Salt

Rapeseed oil, for deep-frying

Chopped fresh coriander
    and/or lime wedges, to serve

1. Cook the onions in the olive oil for 7–8 minutes until tender.

2. Meanwhile, put the grated courgettes into a clean tea towel, roll it up around them then squeeze over a bowl to extract as much moisture as you can – usually a couple of tablespoons or so. Keep this liquid.

3. Mix the squeezed courgettes with 2 tablespoons of the fried onion, the ginger, chopped coriander, chickpea flour and salt to taste. Form the courgette mixture into 16 little balls, roughly the size of walnuts or a bit larger.

4. Put 3cm (1½in) rapeseed oil into a wide saucepan and heat it ready for deep-frying.

5. Keeping an eye on the oil while it's heating, return to your fried onions: add the turmeric, cumin and coriander; stir over the heat for a few seconds, then add the chopped tomatoes, the coconut milk and the reserved courgette liquid. Simmer over a gentle heat.

6. Meanwhile, deep-fry the balls a few at a time until they are deep brown and crisp, about 4–5 minutes. It's really important to cook them long enough to make sure the insides are done, so don't get your oil so hot that they cook too quickly. Drain them on kitchen paper.

7. Pour the sauce into a warmed shallow dish, put the courgette balls in on top, snip over some fresh coriander, and serve. Or serve them on individual plates, in a pool of sauce, with a lime wedge.

Quick and Easy Courgette Tart

I like to use puff pastry made with butter for this, to end up with a lovely light, flaky tart.

Serves 4

375g packet of ready-rolled
   all-butter puff pastry
100g (3½oz) soft goat's cheese
2–4 tbsp water
1 garlic clove, crushed
80g Parmesan-style cheese, grated
350g (12oz) courgettes, thinly sliced
1 tbsp olive oil
Salt and black pepper

1. Preheat the oven to 200°C (400°F), Gas 6.

2. Lay the pastry out on a baking sheet, then score 2cm (¾in) from the edges.

3. Mix the goat's cheese with the water, garlic and half the Parmesan-style cheese, and spread on the pastry, keeping the edges clear.

4. Arrange the thinly sliced courgettes on top, brush with the olive oil, season with salt and pepper, and scatter with the rest of the cheese. Bake for 20 minutes, until puffed up and golden brown.

Tomato and Pesto Tart with a Walnut Crust

This is a beautiful, fast tart, with a crisp walnut crust, topped with pesto, fried onions and juicy ripe tomatoes: the better the tomatoes, the better the tart. Serve it with a salad of summer leaves, and maybe some baby new potatoes. Do try this pastry, even if you never normally make pastry, because it's so easy and so good. You need a large fluted flan dish 24cm (9½in), or something of a similar size, to make it in.

Serves 4

For the walnut pastry

200g (7oz) spelt flour

½ tsp salt

8 tbsp cold-pressed rapeseed oil

2 tbsp water

50g (2oz) walnuts, roughly chopped

For the filling

2–3 tbsp olive oil

2 large onions, finely sliced

3 tbsp pesto
   (see cook's note on page 8)

600g (1lb 6oz) ripe tomatoes,
   thinly sliced

Salt and black pepper

A few fresh basil leaves, to garnish

1. Preheat the oven to 200°C (400°F), Gas 6.

2. Make the pastry: put the flour and salt into a bowl, pour in the oil and water, and mix gently with a fork until it holds together, then stir in the walnuts. Using your fingers, press the mixture into the flan dish, covering the base as evenly as you can, and pushing it up the sides a bit, but you don't need a high crust edge for this. Put into the oven – no need to weigh it down – and bake for 6–8 minutes. Remove from the oven.

3. Meanwhile, heat 1 tablespoon of the olive oil in a pan, add the onions, cover, and cook gently for 10–15 minutes, until tender.

4. Drizzle the pesto over the pastry, then put on the onions in an even layer. Arrange the sliced tomatoes on top, slightly overlapping, to cover the tart completely. Sprinkle with some salt, grind some black pepper over, and drizzle with the remaining olive oil.

5. Put the tart back in the oven and bake for about 8–10 minutes, to cook the tomatoes a little. Scatter with some torn basil leaves and serve.

Chunky Chestnut Sausages

A taste of autumn – Christmas, even – especially if you serve these with Sherry Gravy (see page 149) and some Brussels sprouts. Creamy mash, or Red Cabbage Casserole (see page 166), also go well with them, but kids like them just as they are, or stuffed into a roll, hot-dog style.

Makes 12; serves 4 generously
Vegan

2 tbsp olive oil

2 medium onions, finely chopped

3 celery sticks, finely chopped

2 garlic cloves, crushed

100g (3½oz) wholemeal
    breadcrumbs

435g tin unsweetened
    chestnut purée

2–3 tsp shoyu soy sauce

1–2 tbsp wholemeal flour, for coating

Olive oil, for shallow-frying

1. Heat 1 tablespoon of the oil in a good-sized saucepan, add the onions, celery and garlic, stir, then cover and cook for 5 minutes.

2. Meanwhile, heat the remaining oil in another large saucepan or frying pan, put in the crumbs, and stir over the heat for 4–5 minutes until golden brown.

3. Add the crumbs and chestnut purée to the onion mixture, mix well and season with shoyu to taste.

4. Form into 12 chunky sausages and coat in the flour.

5. Fry in a little rapeseed or olive oil – about a tablespoonful, just enough to 'oil' the pan – turning them so that they get crisp and brown all over. It's easiest to do this if you make them slightly rectangular in shape rather than completely round.

French Bread Pizzas

Crusty bread makes an excellent base for a quick homemade pizza; and French bread, I find, is the best of all because it remains crisp, and tastes the most like a normal pizza. Buy a large, wide baguette or, if you prefer wholemeal, try the crusty round type, sometimes made with added seeds.

Serves 4

1 large, wide French loaf, or a crusty round wholemeal loaf

200g (7oz) feta, crumbled, or mozzarella (not buffalo), torn into pieces

Olive oil, to drizzle

Wild rocket, to serve

For the quick tomato sauce

400g tin chopped tomatoes

1 tsp dried oregano

1 garlic clove, crushed

Salt and black pepper

1. Start with the quick tomato sauce: just put all the ingredients into a saucepan, except the seasoning, and let it bubble over a medium heat until it has reduced by at least half and become thick and rich. Season with salt and pepper.

2. Split the bread in half across and, for the crispest pizza, scoop out some of the crumb. This is optional: keep it if you want a softer, more 'deep pan' effect. Cut your bread into pieces, according to the size you want your pizzas, and what will fit happily under your grill.

3. Spread tomato sauce quite thinly over the top of your 'pizza bases' and cover with toppings (see below).

4. Add the cheese, then put the pizza(s) on a grill pan or baking tin that will fit under your grill and drizzle olive oil around the edges of the bread – this will help it to become crisp.

5. Grill for about 7 minutes, until the topping is hot and lightly browned, and the sides of the pizza are golden brown and crisp.

6. Serve at once. I like to put it on a bed of wild rocket which really complements the hot, crisp pizza and which, strange as it might seem, I find children really love.

A few suggestions for the toppings
Thinly sliced red onions
Red and yellow peppers
Button mushrooms
Marinated barbecued artichoke hearts in oil, drained
Olives, black or green
Sweetcorn
Or anything else you fancy!

Asparagus Frittata with Caper Mayo

A quick-to-make dish for a warm, early summer's day. It's delicious with a salad of crisp lettuce and spring onions.

Serves 4

2 × 350g (12oz) bunches asparagus

2 tbsp olive oil

225g (8oz) grated Cheddar cheese

8 eggs, whisked

Salt and black pepper

For the caper mayo

4 heaped tbsp mayonnaise

1 heaped tbsp tiny capers in vinegar, drained

1. Break off the tough ends of the asparagus by bending the spears until they snap; discard the ends, rinse the rest, then cut the spears in half. Cook them in 1cm (½in) boiling water for 2–5 minutes until just tender. Drain.

2. Heat the oil in a 28cm (11in) frying pan or gratin dish that will go under the grill. Put in the asparagus in an even layer. Sprinkle over half the cheese, then pour the beaten eggs evenly over. Season with salt and pepper, then top with the rest of the cheese.

3. Set the pan over a moderate heat, cover with a lid or a plate and cook for about 5 minutes, or until the base is set and getting browned. Meanwhile, preheat the grill to high.

4. Remove the covering from the pan and put the frittata under the grill for about 10 minutes, or until it has puffed up and browned, and is set in the centre.

5. While the frittata is cooking, mix the mayo with the capers and put into a small bowl.

6. Serve the frittata straight away, with the caper mayo.

Tempeh Flat Cakes

Like tofu, tempeh is a traditional fermented soya protein from Asia, used widely in Indonesian cookery, and can be found in oriental shops and good wholefood shops who know their stuff. These flat cakes are delicious. Try them with some steamed spinach or pak choy, or the Asian Pressed Salad (see page 179).

Serves 2–4 (makes 4 large flat cakes)
Vegan

200g (7oz) block of tempeh,
   plain or with sea vegetables
   (see tip below)
1 tbsp maple syrup
1 tbsp shoyu soy sauce
1 tbsp balsamic vinegar
¼ tsp white pepper
1 medium onion, finely chopped
1 small red pepper,
   deseeded and finely chopped
1 tbsp toasted sesame oil
2 garlic cloves, crushed
50–100g (2–4oz) soft breadcrumbs
Salt and black pepper
Olive or sesame oil,
   for shallow-frying
Lime cut into wedges, to serve

1. Cut the tempeh into thin slices. Put them in a single layer on a plate. Mix together the maple syrup, shoyu, balsamic vinegar and white pepper, and sprinkle this over the slices, as a marinade. Set aside for a few minutes.

2. Fry the onion and red pepper in the oil over a moderate heat, stirring often, for 10 minutes, until tender. Stir in the garlic, cook for a few seconds more, then remove from the heat.

3. Mash the marinated tempeh slices roughly with a fork and add them to the onion and pepper mixture. Add enough breadcrumbs to make the mixture hold together. Season with salt and black pepper.

4. Form the mixture into 4 flat 'cakes', not more than 1cm (½in) thick. Fry them in a little olive or sesame oil. Serve with lime wedges.

Tip: Tempeh comes in a small, flat, vacuum-packed block, from the chill compartment or freezer, and is latte-coloured, with a nubbly texture. You can buy it plain or with various flavourings: I suggest the plain or sea-vegetable one. It's got a really nice, firm, sliceable texture, much more solid than tofu.

Thai-flavoured Chickpea and Millet Cakes with Red Pepper Sauce

Another of those recipes that seem to appeal to everyone; it's easy to make and perfect for a large gathering of all age groups. Along with some salads and dips, it makes for a lovely relaxed meal. Bought Thai curry paste is fine for these but, as always, read the ingredients first to check if it is suitable for vegetarians.

Serves 4

Vegan

125g (4½oz) millet

300ml (11fl oz) water

400g tin chickpeas, drained

3–4 tsp red Thai curry paste, or to taste

4 tbsp chopped fresh coriander

2 spring onions, finely chopped

Salt and black pepper

1–2 tbsp wholemeal flour, to coat

Rapeseed oil, for shallow-frying

For the sweet mustard dip

3 tbsp brown rice syrup or maple syrup

2 tsp Dijon mustard

Good pinch of dried red chilli flakes

For the red pepper sauce

1 red pepper, deseeded and chopped

1 tbsp maple syrup

1 tbsp rice or cider vinegar

Pinch of dried chilli flakes

1. Put the millet into a pan with the water, bring to the boil, cover and cook for 15–20 minutes, until all the water has been absorbed and the millet is light and fluffy.

2. Meanwhile, start the red pepper sauce: put the red pepper into a saucepan with the maple syrup, vinegar and chilli and cook over a gentle heat, covered, for 10–15 minutes, or until the red pepper is very tender. (No need for extra water; the pepper soon produces enough.)

3. Mash the millet and chickpeas together, then mix in the curry paste, coriander, chopped spring onions and salt and pepper to taste.

4. Form the mixture into flat cakes and coat with flour.

5. Heat a little rapeseed oil in a frying pan, then put in the cakes and fry until golden and crisp on both sides, and heated through.

6. While they're frying, make the mustard dip by mixing together the brown rice or maple syrup, the mustard and chilli flakes.

7. Blot the cooked cakes on kitchen paper, and serve with the mustard dip and the red pepper sauce.

Tip: These little cakes freeze brilliantly; so it's well worth doubling the quantities and making more while you're about it. Open-freeze them when you've coated them with flour; they can be quickly shallow-fried from frozen when you need them.

Red Hot Udon Stir-fry

This gorgeous tangle of tender udon noodles, bitter greens, baby mushrooms, onion and red peppers is quick and easy to make, and very filling: a delicious, healthy meal-in-a-bowl. You can buy udon noodles at Asian markets and many supermarkets. I like the Clearspring ones that come in 250g packets, which make the right amount for 4 people.

Serves 4

Vegan

250g packet udon noodles

200g (7oz) ready-to-cook kale

2 tbsp olive oil

1 onion, chopped

1 red pepper, deseeded and chopped

225g (8oz) baby mushrooms, wiped

400g (14oz) pak choy, quartered

2 tomatoes, roughly chopped

1 mild red chilli, deseeded and sliced

3–4 tsp red Thai curry paste
(see tip below)

Salt

2–3 handfuls roasted peanuts,
lightly crushed, to serve

4 lemon wedges, to serve

1. Bring half a large panful of water to the boil and add the noodles. Bring back to the boil and cook for 6–7 minutes, until tender. Drain and leave in a bowl of cold water until needed.

2. Meanwhile, in another pan, cook the kale in 1cm (½in) boiling water, with a lid on the pan, for about 6 minutes, or until tender.

3. Heat the olive oil in a large pan or wok. Put in the onion and red pepper and fry for 5 minutes, then add the mushrooms, pak choy, tomatoes and chilli, toss well, then cover and cook for about 5 minutes, or until all the vegetables are tender.

4. Drain the kale and the udon noodles, and add them to the pan, stirring over the heat.

5. Add a teaspoonful of the Thai curry paste, stir well, taste, and season with salt. Go on adding more curry paste until the mixture is the heat that you like. At this point I sometimes divide it into two pans, so I can make one lot hotter than the rest, depending on who I'm cooking for: some like it hot, some like it milder.

6. Serve immediately on hot plates or in shallow bowls, scatter with crushed peanuts and garnish with a wedge of lemon.

Tip: Make sure the Thai curry paste you use is vegetarian, as many have fish paste in them. I like Por Kwan red curry paste; it comes in a big plastic tub and keeps for ages in the fridge.

Deep-fried Tofu with Lemon

If you fancy a taste of the sea, but don't want to eat fish, try this for an indulgent treat. Serve it with wedges of lemon, and make more of a meal of it with a lightly cooked green vegetable.

Serves 4

Vegan

Rapeseed oil, for deep-frying

394g block of tofu

1 sheet of nori

Lemon wedges, to serve

For the batter

50g (2oz) plain white flour

100g (3½oz) cornflour

¼ tsp salt

1½ tsp baking powder

About 200ml (7fl oz) sparkling water

1. Half-fill one or two woks, deep-frying pans or large heavy saucepans with rapeseed oil. Heat until a small cube of bread sizzles and rises to the surface immediately and browns in 1 minute.

2. While the oil is heating, mix the batter: put the flours, salt and baking powder into a bowl, add the sparkling water and mix quickly using a fork or chopstick; it needs to remain a bit lumpy and some bits of flour don't matter. You need a thickish batter that will cling to the tofu when you dip it in: you can add a bit more water or cornflour to adjust if necessary.

3. Drain the tofu but don't dry it. Cut across into slices about 8mm (¼in) thick so that you get about 12 from the block. Cut the nori into similar-sized rectangles: you should get 12 from a sheet.

4. When the oil is hot, lay a piece of nori on one side of a piece of tofu, dip in the batter, being careful not to dislodge the nori, let any excess batter drip off, then gently drop the battered tofu into the oil. Let it cook for about 3–4 minutes, or until it is golden brown (not too dark), and crisp, then carefully lift it out with a slotted spoon and drain it on kitchen paper. You can add more while the first is cooking, but make sure you attach the nori and dip the tofu in the batter immediately before frying, so the nori doesn't get soggy.

5. Serve with lemon wedges.

Black Sesame-coated Tofu Triangles with Noodles and Pak Choy

This is a delicious dish full of contrasts: tender tofu coated with crunchy, black sesame seeds served with soft, comforting noodles and bright pak choy and spring onions. Black sesame seeds can be found in Asian shops and good wholefood stores. You can use them in any recipe that calls for sesame seeds: the flavour is similar to that of the beige ones, or the more widely available white ones that have had their hulls removed.

Serves 4

Vegan

493g firm tofu, drained, blotted on kitchen paper and cut into small triangles not more than 6mm (¼in) thick

For the marinade and coating

3 tbsp shoyu soy sauce

2 tbsp cider vinegar

1 tbsp olive oil

1 tbsp ume seasoning, if available (see tip on page 84)

¼ tsp salt

¼ tsp ground white pepper

4 tbsp wholemeal flour

4 tbsp black sesame seeds

Olive oil, for frying

For the noodles

250g packet of udon noodles

400g (14oz) pak choy, roughly chopped

2 tbsp toasted sesame oil

6 spring onions, chopped

1. Make the marinade: put the soy sauce, cider vinegar, olive oil, ume seasoning, if you're using it, salt and pepper on to a large plate and mix gently. Put the tofu on to the plate on top of the marinade and leave for 10 minutes, turning the pieces at half time.

2. Cook the noodles in water according to the packet directions, until they're almost done. Drain them into a sieve and refresh under cold water.

3. Bring 1cm (½in) water to the boil in a large saucepan and cook the pak choy for 2–3 minutes until tender; drain into a colander.

4. Finish the tofu: spread the wholemeal flour and black sesame seeds and a good pinch of salt out on a large plate. Take the pieces of tofu out of the marinade, shaking off any excess. Coat the pieces of tofu on both sides with the flour and sesame mixture, pressing the coating firmly to help it to stick. Reserve any leftover marinade.

5. Shallow-fry the tofu in a little olive oil until crisp and lightly browned; you may have to do this in two batches; keep the first ones warm while you finish the rest.

6. While the tofu is frying, heat the toasted sesame oil in a large saucepan, add the drained noodles, pak choy, reserved marinade and chopped spring onions, and stir-fry over a gentle heat for a few minutes to warm everything through. Season with salt and pepper.

7. Serve the noodle mixture on warmed plates and top with the triangles of tofu.

Kerala Curry

A long list of ingredients, but an easy method: this curry is full of flavour and colour. Serve it with plain boiled rice. If there's any left over, it heats up well and, like many spicy dishes, is even better the next day.

Serves 6

Vegan

3 tbsp olive oil

300g (11oz) finely chopped onions

300g (11oz) sliced carrots

300g (11oz) sliced new potatoes

300g (11oz) sliced cauliflower florets

300g (11oz) green beans in 5cm
   lengths

1 green chilli, deseeded, sliced

400ml tin coconut milk

Salt and pepper

Small bunch of fresh coriander,
   chopped, to serve

For the dry spice mix

1½ tsp each of chilli powder,
   ground coriander, fennel seed
   and turmeric

Seeds from 6 cardamom pods,
   crushed

For the wet spice mix

300g (11oz) tomatoes, chopped

6 garlic cloves, peeled

6cm (2½in) fresh ginger, peeled

1. Start by making the wet spice mix: purée the ingredients in a food processor or with a hand-held blender; set aside.

2. Heat the oil in a large saucepan, add the onions, carrots and potatoes, and cook gently, covered, but stir occasionally, for 10 minutes, until beginning to soften.

3. Stir in the dry spices, cook for a minute or so until they smell fragrant, then add the cauliflower, green beans, chilli and the wet spice mix. Stir, and cook gently for 10 minutes, until the vegetables are pretty well tender.

4. Pour in the coconut milk and heat gently. Add salt and pepper to taste, scatter with chopped coriander, and serve.

Roasted Aubergine in Tomato Sauce with Melted Mozzarella

Tender slices of aubergine, tomato sauce with its herby, sunshine flavours, and oozing, melting mozzarella: and so easy to make. Try adding a handful of black olives, and/or some drained and rinsed capers to the tomato sauce for extra zing.

Serves 4

2 medium aubergines,
    cut into 8cm (3in) slices
Olive oil
200g (7oz) mozzarella cheese
    (see tip below), sliced

For the tomato sauce

2 onions, chopped
1 tbsp olive oil
4 garlic cloves, finely chopped
2 × 400g tins chopped tomatoes
Salt and pepper

1. Brush the slices of aubergine on both sides with olive oil. Lay the pieces in a single layer on a grill pan or in a tin that will fit under your grill, and grill for about 3 minutes on each side, or until tender but not browned. You may have to do this in two batches.

2. Meanwhile, make the sauce. Fry the onions in the oil with a lid on the pan for about 8 minutes, until almost tender. Add the garlic and cook for a further 2 minutes, then put in the tomatoes and cook over a brisk heat, uncovered, for 10 minutes or until very thick.

3. Season the aubergine slices with salt and pepper and put them into a shallow dish that will fit under your grill. Top the aubergine with the tomato sauce; and put the cheese on top of that.

4. Grill for about 10 minutes, or until the cheese has melted and is golden brown.

Tip: Vegetarian mozzarella is widely available in supermarkets, though you won't find it amongst the buffalo mozzarellas, because these are made according to traditional methods with animal rennet.

Food for
Family & Friends

Rendang Malaysian Vegetable and Coconut Curry

This is a rich, coconutty curry that is delicious with plain boiled rice and a pile of fast-cooked baby spinach leaves. Add the chilli according to your taste; if not everyone you're cooking for likes it hot, you could do what I tend to do and use dried chilli flakes, adding them to part of the curry at the end.

Serves 4

Vegan

For the curry paste

3 tbsp desiccated coconut

2 garlic cloves, peeled

1 onion, sliced

2 stalks lemongrass, tough outer part removed, inside sliced

1–3 fresh red chillies, deseeded, or hot red chilli flakes to taste, see above

Piece of fresh ginger the size of a large walnut, peeled and roughly sliced

1 tsp turmeric

Salt

1 tsp sugar

2 tbsp olive oil

400ml tin coconut milk

1 tsp tamarind pulp from a jar

4 star anise

1 cinnamon stick

1 lime, halved

For the vegetables

250g (9oz) carrots, cut into thin rings

200g (7oz) tender cabbage, such pointed white cabbage, shredded

100g (3½oz) frozen petits pois, thawed

2 tbsp chopped fresh coriander, to serve

4 tbsp salted peanuts, crushed, to serve

1. The carrots need to be parboiled ready to add to the curry, so start by bringing 1cm (½in) water to the boil in a saucepan, put in the carrots, cover and cook for about 10 minutes, or until just tender.

2. Meanwhile, put the desiccated coconut into a dry frying pan and stir over the heat for just a moment or two until it turns slightly golden, then take it off the heat immediately and tip it straight into a food processor, or a deep bowl or goblet suitable for using a hand-held blender in. You need to be speedy to make sure the coconut doesn't go on cooking in the hot pan, and get too brown.

3. Add to the food processor, or deep bowl, the garlic, onion, lemongrass, chillies – or add these separately at the end to just part of the curry, if not everyone likes it hot – ginger, turmeric, 1 teaspoon salt and sugar, and whizz to a thick paste.

4. Heat the oil in the frying pan (which needs to be deep – otherwise use a wide saucepan) and add the paste you've just made; stir for a couple of minutes to cook the spices, then add the coconut milk, tamarind, star anise and cinnamon stick, and bring to the boil, stirring. Reduce the heat and let it cook gently for 5 minutes.

5. Drain the carrots and add to the curry, along with the cabbage; let the curry continue to cook gently for 10 minutes, until the vegetables are tender, and the curry is thick and glossy. Add the petits pois, cook for a further few minutes to heat them through.

6. Taste the curry and add some lime juice and salt as necessary. Serve scattered with the chopped coriander and crushed peanuts.

Thai Stir-fry

This is a fast stir-fry made with bought Thai curry paste. The secret to getting a fresh taste is the fast cooking of the vegetables, and the generous scattering of chopped coriander over the top. It's delicious with some plain boiled rice; put this on to cook first of all.

Serves 4

Vegan

2 tbsp olive oil

2 large carrots, cut into thin rounds

2 red peppers, deseeded
    and thinly sliced

250g (9oz) mangetout,
    halved lengthways

250g (9oz) baby sweetcorn,
    sliced on the diagonal

300g (11oz) baby mushrooms,
    halved as necessary

1 bunch of spring onions,
    trimmed and sliced

4 tsp red Thai curry paste,
    or to taste (see tip on page 108)

400ml tin coconut milk

Small bunch fresh coriander

Salt and black pepper

For the rice

300g (11oz) white basmati rice,
    well rinsed

400ml (14fl oz) water

1. Start with the rice: put the rice into a heavy-based pan with the water. Bring to the boil, put a lid on the pan, and reduce the heat to a low simmer. Set a timer for 14 minutes. As soon as the time is up, take the pan off the heat, without removing the lid (this is important!), and let it stand for another 8 minutes, to steam in its own heat.

2. For the curry, heat the oil in a wok or very large saucepan and add the carrots and red peppers; let them cook gently, with a lid on the pan, for about 3 minutes, stirring so they don't stick, then add the rest of the vegetables. Stir so they are coated with the oil, then cover and cook for 2–3 minutes, until they have softened a bit.

3. Put the curry paste in a bowl and gradually stir in the coconut milk until they are smooth and well blended, then pour this into the pan.

4. Bring to the boil, then turn the heat down and let the curry simmer gently for 2–3 minutes, or until the vegetables are glistening and the right degree of tenderness for you.

5. Check the seasoning, snip the fresh coriander generously over the top, and serve with the hot cooked rice.

Marinated Tofu with Purple Sprouting Broccoli and Tahini Sauce

This is gorgeous: a heap of brown basmati rice piled up with bright green broccoli spears and crisp, sizzling tofu drizzled with creamy tahini sauce scattered with toasted hazelnuts and bright green flecks of flat-leaf parsley. It's definitely got the wow factor.

Serves 4
Vegan

394g block tofu, drained, blotted and cut into rectangles not more than 6mm (¼in) thick

400g (14oz) brown basmati rice, rinsed

1 litre (1¾ pints) boiling water

Olive oil, for shallow-frying

200g (7oz) trimmed purple sprouting broccoli (see page 172 for more about this)

4 tbsp crushed toasted hazelnuts, to serve

4 tbsp chopped flat-leaf parsley, to serve

For the marinade and coating

3 tbsp shoyu soy sauce

2 tbsp cider vinegar

1 tbsp olive oil

1 tbsp ume seasoning, if available (see tip on page 84)

¼ tsp salt

¼ tsp ground white pepper

4–5 tbsp wholemeal flour

Pinch of salt

For the tahini sauce

4 tbsp tahini

1 garlic clove, crushed

1–2 tsp lemon juice

Pinch of salt

4–5 tbsp water

1. Make the marinade: put the soy sauce, cider vinegar, olive oil, ume seasoning, if you're using it, salt and pepper on to a large plate and mix gently. Put the tofu on a plate with the marinade and leave for 10–15 minutes, turning the pieces at half time.

2. Meanwhile, put the rice and boiling water into a saucepan, bring back to the boil, then cover, turn down the heat and leave to cook gently for 25 minutes, or until all the water has been absorbed and the rice is tender.

3. Make the tahini sauce: put the tahini, garlic, lemon juice and salt into a bowl and gradually stir in the water, to make a lovely pale creamy sauce. Set aside.

4. Finish the tofu: spread the wholemeal flour and salt out on a large plate. Take the pieces of tofu out of the marinade, shake off any excess. Coat them on both sides with the flour. Reserve any leftover marinade.

5. Heat a little olive oil in a frying pan. Fry the slices of tofu over a fairly high heat until they are brown and sticky on one side, then turn them over.

6. While the tofu is frying, heat 1cm (½in) water in a large saucepan, add the broccoli and cook, covered, for 4–6 minutes, or until tender, then drain and keep warm.

7. When the tofu is brown and sticky on both sides, remove from the pan. Reheat the remaining marinade.

8. Divide the cooked rice between 4 plates. Pile the broccoli and tofu on top. Spoon over the marinade and drizzle with the tahini sauce. Scatter with the toasted hazelnuts and chopped parsley, and serve.

Tip: The thinner you cut the tofu, the better it absorbs the marinade and the crisper it fries.

Quick Dosa Masala with Fresh Tomato Chutney

Normally these crisp Indian pancakes are made from a purée of lentils and rice that is fermented overnight: hardly a 30-minute recipe! This quick version uses chickpea and white self-raising flour and tastes just as delicious. I have four tips for getting the pancakes perfect: make sure the batter is really thin; use a wide, non-stick frying pan; have it really hot and the base covered with oil; and when you pour the batter in, tilt the frying pan so that it runs all over the base, as it won't spread by itself.

Makes 4 big pancakes

Vegan

For the masala filling

500g (1lb 2oz) potatoes, peeled and cut into 2cm (¾in) cubes

2 tbsp olive oil

1 tsp cumin seeds

2 onions, finely chopped

1 tsp finely grated fresh ginger

2 garlic cloves, crushed

1 green chilli, deseeded and finely chopped

½ tsp turmeric

1 tsp salt

2 tbsp chopped fresh coriander

For the dosa

50g (2oz) chickpea flour

50g (2oz) white self-raising flour

¼ tsp salt

2 tsp black or brown mustard seeds (optional)

250ml (9fl oz) cold water

Olive oil, for frying

For the fresh tomato chutney

2 tomatoes, chopped

1 small onion, chopped

Juice of 1 lime

1. First prepare the filling. Boil the potatoes in 1cm (½in) water, covered, until tender.

2. Heat the oil in a frying pan, add the cumin seeds and stir over the heat for a few seconds. When they pop, add the onions. Cook for 5 minutes, then put in the ginger, garlic, chilli, turmeric and salt, and cook for a further 5 minutes. Add the warm potatoes, and gently fold through. Set aside.

3. To make the chutney, mix the tomatoes with the onion, lime juice and some salt. Put into a small bowl and set aside.

4. To make the dosa, put the chickpea flour into a bowl and mix to break up any lumps, then add the self-raising flour and salt, and the mustard seeds, if using, and gradually stir in the water, to make a thin batter.

5. When you're ready to make the dosa, heat 2 tablespoons olive oil in a wide non-stick frying pan. When it's smoking hot, tip in some batter, swirling the pan as you do, so that the batter runs all over the base and even a little up the sides, coating it really thinly.

6. Let the pancake cook for a minute or two – lift the edges with a spatula to see how it's cooking; it needs to be a deep, golden brown. Then turn it over with a fish slice, and cook the other side briefly. Make 3 more dosa.

7. While the dosa are cooking, gently reheat the potato filling and stir in the chopped coriander.

8. Spoon the filling on top of the dosas and gently roll them over. Serve immediately, with the fresh tomato chutney.

Vegetable Curry with Bombay Potatoes and Dal

When all my family descend on me in large numbers, ages ranging from my two-year-old grandson to my nonagenarian aunt, and I want to please them all, this is what I make: three different curries from one basic spicy mixture. There are lots of pans involved, and you'll be busy all the time, but it can be achieved in 30 minutes as long as you've done your prepping first. The curries are quite mild – to suit all palates – but they can be revved up with additional dried red chilli flakes to taste.

Serves 6

Vegan

For the basic sauce

1 tbsp olive oil

2 onions, finely chopped

2 garlic, chopped

2 tbsp grated fresh ginger

1 tsp turmeric

1 tsp paprika

1 tsp ground cumin

1 tsp garam masala

½–1 tsp chilli powder

1 tsp salt

400g tin chopped tomatoes

400ml (14fl oz) water

For the dal

200g (7oz) split red lentils

800ml (29fl oz) water

1 tbsp olive oil

4 garlic cloves, sliced

1 tsp black or brown mustard seeds

1. Start with the dal: put the lentils and water into a deep pan, bring to the boil, and leave to simmer until the lentils are tender: 15–20 minutes.

2. For the basic sauce, heat the oil in a large pan, add the onions, garlic and ginger and cook for 5 minutes until the onions are softening.

3. Meanwhile get the potatoes and the cauliflower on to cook, in separate pans, the potatoes with water to almost cover, and the cauliflower in 2cm (¾in) water. Cover them and leave to simmer until tender – the cauliflower will need 8–10 minutes, the potatoes about 15 minutes.

4. Once they're on, come back to the pan with the onions and add the turmeric, paprika, cumin, garam masala, chilli powder and salt. Stir over the heat for a few moments, until aromatic, then remove from the heat and add the tomatoes and water. Blend with a hand-held blender, or in a food processor, until very smooth. Reheat the mixture in its original pan, letting it simmer over a gentle heat for 15 minutes.

5. Drain the potatoes and the cauliflower and return them to their pans. Divide the curry sauce into three portions: add one to the potatoes, one to the cauliflower, along with the petits pois, and one to the dal, stirring well. Put them all back on the heat, season with salt and pepper, and keep them warm until you're ready to serve.

For the Bombay potatoes

750g (1lb 10oz) potatoes, peeled
  and cut into 1cm (½in) cubes
2–3 tbsp fresh coriander, chopped

For the vegetable curry

1 medium cauliflower,
  divided into small florets
150g (5oz) frozen petits pois, thawed
2 tomatoes, chopped

6. To finish the dal, heat the oil in a small saucepan, add the sliced garlic, and fry for a few seconds until it begins to brown and crisp, then add the mustard seeds and fry for a few more seconds until they start to pop. Pour the sizzling mixture over the top of the dal.

7. Scatter the chopped coriander over the top of the Bombay potatoes. Garnish the cauliflower curry with the chopped tomato. Serve the three curries in separate warmed bowls for guests to help themselves.

Tip: The basic curry sauce freezes beautifully, which allows you to make it in advance, if you'd like to be as organised as that. It's very good with Turmeric Rice (see page 152).

Stuffed Squash with Walnuts and Goat's Cheese

This looks and tastes lovely. It looks best, and cooks quickest, if you cut the solid 'neck' of the butternut squash off. To save wasting that part, you could cook it in the oven at the same time, leaving it in a bit longer to become fully tender, and keep it for another recipe. Wilted spinach makes a really good accompaniment.

Serves 4

2 medium-sized butternut squash, halved, seeds scooped out, 'neck' end cut off

2 tbsp olive oil

150g (5oz) brown basmati and wild rice mix, rinsed

250ml (9fl oz) water

1 large or 2 medium red onions, sliced

2 garlic cloves, crushed

1 lemon, halved

50g (2oz) walnuts, roughly chopped

175g (6oz) firm goat's cheese, cubed

Salt and black pepper

1. Preheat the oven to 220°C (425°F), Gas 7.

2. Brush the butternut squash, inside and out, with 1 tablespoon of the olive oil; season with a little salt. Put in a roasting tin, skin-side down, and roast for 25 minutes, or until tender to the point of a knife.

3. Meanwhile, make the stuffing. Put the rice into a saucepan with the water, bring to the boil, then cover and leave to cook undisturbed over a gentle heat for 20–25 minutes, until the rice is tender and all the water has been absorbed.

4. Heat the remaining tablespoon of olive oil in a pan, and cook the red onion over a gentle heat for 7–8 minutes, then add the crushed garlic and cook for 1–2 minutes. Remove from the heat.

5. Stir the cooked rice with a fork, then mix in the cooked red onion and garlic, 1 tablespoon freshly squeezed lemon juice, the walnuts and goat's cheese. Season well with salt and pepper.

6. Pile the stuffing mixture into the cavities of the 4 butternut squash halves. Serve at once, or pop back into the oven for 5 minutes to melt the goat's cheese a bit if you prefer.

Pointed Red Peppers Stuffed with Artichoke Hearts and Feta

To me these taste of sunshine, and they couldn't be easier to do. Serve them with crusty bread or quickly made couscous, and a green salad, for a fast, delicious meal.

Serves 4

4 pointed red peppers, halved through the stalks, cores and seeds removed

200g (7oz) barbecued artichokes in oil, drained, oil reserved

200g (7oz) feta cheese, roughly crumbled or cubed

300g (11oz) small cherry tomatoes, or larger ones, halved

24 black olives, such as Kalamata

A handful of fresh basil leaves, roughly torn

1. Preheat the oven to 230ºC (450ºF), Gas 9.

2. Lay the peppers side by side in a shallow gratin or roasting tin. Divide the artichoke hearts, feta, cherry tomatoes and olives between the peppers. Bake for 15–20 minutes, or until the peppers are tender and the ingredients lightly browned.

3. Scatter with fresh basil, and serve.

Griddled Mediterranean Vegetables with Couscous, Hummus and Toasted Pine Nuts

The secret to making this in 30 minutes is having a large enough griddle; really, to do it for 4 people in 30 minutes you need 2 large ridged frying pans, or, if not, just cook the vegetables in more batches, and allow an extra few minutes accordingly. It's delicious: full of colour and sunshine flavours, one of my favourite simple meals.

Serves 4

Vegan

1 large aubergine, cut lengthways into slices 8mm (¼in) thick

1 red onion, cut into wedges or thick rounds

1 red pepper, deseeded and cut into rectangular pieces

1 yellow pepper, deseeded and cut into rectangular pieces

2 large courgettes, cut into thick slices

1–2 bunches of asparagus, tough ends removed

4 tomatoes, halved

Olive oil

For the couscous

250g (9oz) couscous

500ml (18fl oz) boiling water

To serve

Hummus, bought or homemade (see page 59)

Toasted pine nuts

Chopped flat-leaf parsley

Lemon wedges

1. Preheat the oven to 150°C (300°F), Gas 2, for keeping the vegetables warm as they're ready.

2. Heat 1 or 2 griddles. Except for the peppers, you will need to oil the vegetables. A quick way to do this is to pour a thin layer of olive oil on to a large plate and quickly dip the vegetables into it just before you put them on the griddle.

3. Cook the vegetables in the order given in the ingredients list, putting as many as you can slantwise on to the griddle, without overlapping them. When the first side has become marked with lovely deep brown stripes, turn the pieces over and do the second side. When that is done transfer them to a roasting tin and keep warm in the oven. Continue like this until all the vegetables are cooked.

4. While the vegetables are cooking, you will have time to prepare the couscous: put into a bowl, cover with boiling water and leave until all the water has been absorbed. Fork through and season with a little salt and scatter with chopped parsley.

5. Serve the vegetables on warmed individual plates or on a large platter, with the couscous, the hummus scattered with toasted pine nuts, the chopped parsley and lemon wedges.

Stuffed Brandied Field Mushrooms

This special dish was inspired by the wonderful mushrooms that Rachel Demuth serves at her charming vegetarian restaurant in Bath at Christmas. For the complete Christmas experience, some Brussels sprouts go really well with this (see recipe on page 175). Mine perch proudly on top of rösti cakes. You can do all of this in 30 minutes, but you will need four 9cm (4in) metal rings for cooking the rösti and a frying pan that is wide enough to hold them.

Serves 4

Vegan

4 large field or Portobello
    mushrooms, wiped
3 tbsp olive oil
2 tbsp brandy
Salt and black pepper

For the stuffing

75g (3oz) brown basmati rice, rinsed
75ml (3fl oz) red wine
75ml (3fl oz) water
1 tsp vegetable stock powder
1 onion, chopped
200g (7oz) peeled and deseeded
    butternut squash, cut into 1cm
    (½in) cubes
2 garlic cloves, crushed
Large sprig of rosemary, leaves
    roughly chopped
2 sage leaves, chopped
Bunch of flat-leaf parsley, chopped
25g (1oz) pine nuts, toasted
Salt and black pepper

For the rösti

800g grated potatoes, squeezed
    in a clean tea towel to make
    them as dry as possible
A little balsamic reduction, to glaze,
    (see page 64, optional)

1. Preheat the oven to 200°C (400°F), Gas 6.

2. Start with the stuffing: put the rice, red wine, water and stock powder into a pan, bring to the boil, then cover and leave to cook over a low heat for 20–25 minutes, until all the water has been absorbed and the rice is tender.

3. Put the mushrooms stalk-side up in a roasting tin and drizzle with 1 tablespoon of the olive oil and the brandy. Season with salt and pepper, cover lightly with foil and bake for 20–25 minutes, until tender.

4. Meanwhile make the rösti: heat 1 tablespoon of the olive oil in a large frying pan. Position four 9cm (4in) metal rings, oiled inside, in the frying pan. Season the grated potato with salt, then divide between the metal rings, packing it in firmly. Leave over the heat for about 5 minutes, until golden brown, then carefully turn over the rings and their filling (you might need to push the potato down a bit so that it makes contact with the frying pan) to cook through and brown the second side, which will take about 5–10 minutes.

5. Heat the remaining 1 tablespoon of olive oil in a medium-large pan, add the onion, butternut squash and garlic, cover and cook over a fairly gentle heat for 10 minutes, or until the butternut squash is just tender. Remove from the heat.

6. Add the cooked rice to the butternut squash mixture, along with the chopped rosemary, sage, parsley and half the pine nuts. Season with salt and pepper.

continues overleaf

7. To serve, put a rösti circle on each plate. Top with a mushroom and pile each mushroom with a quarter of the stuffing. Divide the remaining pine nuts between them. If you want to get all 'cheffy', drizzle a little balsamic glaze around the plate, then serve at once.

Tip: You can buy balsamic glaze, but it's really easy to make your own purer version with just balsamic vinegar and maple syrup (see the recipe on page 64). It will keep for weeks.

Grilled Garlic Mushroom Skewers

Everyone loves garlic mushrooms and these skewers – which can be cooked on a barbecue or under the grill – are gorgeous. Scoop the oozy, salty, garlicky mushrooms into wholemeal pitta breads, or warm ciabatta, and eat with your hands.

Makes 8 skewers

Vegan

500g (1lb 2oz), or about 80, baby
    mushrooms, washed and patted dry

Roughly chopped flat-leaf parsley,
    to serve

For the garlic and olive oil paste

2 tbsp crushed garlic – you can use
    'lazy garlic' to save time here

4 tbsp olive oil

2 tbsp freshly squeezed lemon juice

½ tsp sea salt

1. Thread the mushrooms on to the skewers, packing them as close together as you can because they will shrink during cooking.

2. Make the paste by mixing all the ingredients together, then rub it over all the mushrooms.

3. Grill or barbecue the mushroom skewers for about 10 minutes, or until golden brown and tender.

4. Scatter with fresh flat-leaf parsley and serve at once.

Baked Stuffed Avocados

This is rich but wonderful, with lots of contrasting flavours and textures. The most important thing is to use avocados that are just ripe, and only cook them long enough to warm them through, to preserve their delicate flavour. Serve them with something fresh and simple, such as wilted spinach or a pretty leaf salad with a very light dressing.

Serves 4

Vegan

2 large ripe avocados

4 spring onions, chopped

1 tsp curry powder

60g (2½oz) salted macadamias
   or cashews

100g (3½oz) Cheddar cheese, diced

4 tbsp grated Parmesan-style cheese

Salt and black pepper

1. Preheat the oven to 200ºC (400ºF), Gas 6.

2. Halve and stone the avocados, and scoop out the flesh with a teaspoon, being careful not to damage the skins. Dice the flesh roughly.

3. Add the spring onions to the avocado flesh, together with the curry powder, nuts and Cheddar cheese. Season with salt and pepper.

4. Pile the mixture back into the avocado skins, scatter the grated cheese over the top and place, uncovered, in a shallow ovenproof dish. Bake for 10–15 minutes, until warmed through and lightly browned on top. Serve at once.

Grilled Halloumi Skewers with Red and Yellow Peppers and Herby Couscous

Whether cooked on a barbecue or in the kitchen under the grill, these colourful skewers really bring the sunshine with them! The marinade adds just that right note of sweet-tanginess. Instead of herby couscous, you could serve the skewers in pitta pockets.

Makes 8 skewers

2 red peppers, deseeded and cut into thin strips

2 yellow peppers, deseeded and cut into thin strips

32 fresh bay leaves

2 × 250g packets of halloumi cheese, cut into 20 pieces each

For the marinade

4 tbsp tomato ketchup

2 tbsp honey

4 garlic cloves, crushed

2 tbsp olive oil

2 tbsp shoyu soy sauce

1 tbsp wine vinegar

For the herby couscous

500ml (18fl oz) vegetable stock

250g (9oz) couscous

1 tbsp olive oil

4 tbsp chopped fresh herbs

Salt and pepper

Lemon wedges, to serve

1. To make the skewers, thread alternating red and yellow pepper slices, bay leaves and pieces of halloumi on to skewers. Put them in a single layer in a shallow container like a roasting tin.

2. Make the marinade by mixing all the ingredients together. Pour over the skewers, turning them to make sure everything gets coated. Set aside until about 10 minutes before you want to eat.

3. Meanwhile, prepare the couscous. Bring the stock to the boil, add the couscous and olive oil. Cover and set aside, off the heat, for 10–15 minutes.

4. About 10 minutes before you want to eat, place the skewers under the grill, or over a barbecue on top of a fine mesh grid. Cook them for about 5 minutes on one side, then turn them over and cook the other side, until the cheese is golden-brown and the peppers are charred in places and beginning to soften.

5. Add the herbs to the couscous, gently forking them through. Season with salt and pepper and serve with the skewers, with lemon wedges on the side.

Make it vegan: With this strong, sweet marinade, you can easily use tofu instead of halloumi, for a vegan version; it will soak up the flavours and taste great. Use maple or rice syrup instead of honey in the marinade.

Creamy Leek Tart

This is such a lovely combination: crisp, nutty-tasting wholemeal pastry, silky, creamy leeks, and the salty tang of capers. I used an ordinary 20cm (8in) metal flan tin with 3cm (1¼in) sides for this, and it was perfect. I like to make my own pastry – it's really quick and easy – but you could use bought shortcrust if you prefer. Serve with some salad and baby new potatoes, or mash if you want something more substantial.

Serves 4

2 tbsp olive oil

500g (1lb 2oz) trimmed thin leeks, sliced

1 tbsp cornflour

250ml (9fl oz) single cream

1 tsp Dijon mustard

3 tbsp capers, rinsed and drained

Salt and black pepper

4–5 caper berries, to serve

For the pastry

200g (7oz) spelt flour

½ tsp salt

8 tbsp cold-pressed rapeseed oil

2 tbsp water

1. Preheat the oven to 200ºC (400ºF), Gas 6.

2. Heat the olive oil in a large pan, add the leeks, stir, then cover and cook over a gentle heat, without letting them brown, for 7–10 minutes, or until tender.

3. Meanwhile, make the pastry: put the flour and salt into a bowl, pour in the oil and water, and mix gently with a fork until it holds together.

4. Form the pastry into a ball, place on a piece of cling film, flatten it with the palm of your hand, then place another piece of cling film on top. Roll the pastry out between the two pieces of cling film, giving it a quarter turn every so often, to make a circle that fits the flan tin.

5. Peel off the top piece of cling film then invert the pastry over the flan tin and press it into place. Peel off the remaining piece of cling film, trim the edges of the pastry and prick the base. Bake for 6–8 minutes, until crisp and lightly browned.

6. Meanwhile, finish the filling. In a small bowl mix the cornflour with a little of the single cream to make a smooth paste. Bring the rest of the cream to the boil, pour over the cornflour in the bowl, stir, then return to the pan and stir over a gentle heat for a minute or two until the mixture thickens. Stir in the mustard, capers and salt and pepper to taste.

7. Drain the leeks, and combine gently with the cream mixture – leave some chunky pieces of leek showing.

8. Spoon the leek mixture into the pastry case then put it back into the oven for 4–5 minutes to lightly brown the top. Put the caper berries on top as a garnish, and serve.

Tip: Any left over reheats really well, but it's also lovely cold. And it freezes well after cooking. To use, thaw, then reheat.

Make it vegan: For a dairy-free version, this is delicious made with unsweetened vegan single cream.

Gratin Dauphinois

Normally this would take at least an hour, if not longer, to cook in the oven, but I've found that you can make it in just 30 minutes if you boil sliced potatoes in water until tender, then layer them with cream and brown them under a grill for about 15 minutes. Perfect when you want something special and comforting in a hurry – and you can even make a lovely vegan version too. Serve with a great salad, like the Baby Spinach, Apple, Celery and Hazelnut on page 164, or with buttery spinach or green beans and grilled tomatoes.

Serves 4

1.3kg (3lb) peeled waxy potatoes such as Maris Piper, sliced not more than 5mm (¼in) thick

4 tbsp olive oil

300ml (11fl oz) double cream

2 large garlic cloves, crushed

Salt, grated nutmeg and black pepper

1. Cook the potato slices in 1cm (½in) water in a wide saucepan, covered, for 7–10 minutes or until you can pierce them with the point of a knife.

2. Drain off the water and add to the pan 2 tablespoons of the olive oil, the double cream, and a good seasoning of salt, grated nutmeg and black pepper, moving the potato slices gently so that they get well coated.

3. Use some of the remaining olive oil to grease a shallow ovenproof dish that will fit under your grill, then put in the potatoes, levelling them off, and pour the remaining tablespoon of olive oil over the top.

4. Cook under a hot grill for about 15 minutes, or until golden brown and a bit crisp on top, and heated right through.

Make it vegan: For an excellent vegan version use a 275ml carton of single soya cream instead of the dairy cream.

Red Onion Tarts

You can just get these made, pastry and all, in 30 minutes! I like to make my own pastry with wholemeal spelt flour and healthy cold-pressed golden rapeseed oil, but you could use bought shortcrust if you prefer. You'll need four 10cm (4in) shallow metal flan tins for these, though these quantities are also right for a shallow 20cm (8in) flan tin if you'd prefer to make one larger one. Serve as a starter, with a little salad garnish; or with baby new potatoes, or mash, and green beans or a pretty salad, as a main course.

Serves 4

500g (1lb 2oz) red onions, finely sliced

1 tbsp olive oil

1 tbsp balsamic vinegar

100g (3½oz) firm goat's cheese, flaked

Salt

For the pastry

200g (7oz) spelt flour

½ tsp salt

8 tbsp cold-pressed rapeseed oil

2 tbsp water

Sprigs of rosemary, to serve

1. Preheat the oven to 200ºC (400ºF), Gas 6.

2. Get the onions on to cook: heat the oil in a large saucepan, add the onions, stir, cover and cook gently for about 15 minutes, stirring occasionally, then add the balsamic vinegar and season with salt. Keep warm over a gentle heat.

3. Meanwhile, make the flan cases: put the flour and salt into a bowl, pour in the oil and water, and mix gently with a fork until it holds together.

4. Divide the pastry into 4 equal pieces and form each into a ball. Roll each out between two pieces of cling film, giving it a quarter turn every so often, making the pastry as thin as possible – the cling film really helps here.

5. Peel off the top piece of cling film then invert the pastry over a flan tin and press it into place. Peel off the remaining piece of cling film, trim the edges of the pastry and prick the base. Repeat with the remaining flans. Bake for 6–8 minutes, until crisp and lightly browned. Preheat the grill.

6. Spoon the balsamic onions into the cases, sprinkle with goat's cheese, grill for about 5 minutes or until the cheese has melted and lightly browned and serve with a sprig of rosemary.

Spinach Tagliatelle with Walnuts

This is a rich pasta dish, which only needs a simple salad accompaniment: a fresh tomato and basil salad or a green salad, such as oak-leaf lettuce, with a very light dressing.

Serves 4

25g (1oz) butter
1 large onion, chopped
2 garlic cloves, crushed
300ml (11fl oz) double cream
400g (14oz) spinach tagliatelle
50–75g (2–3oz) walnuts, chopped
Salt and black pepper

1. First fill a saucepan with 2 litres (3½ pints) of water and bring to the boil for the pasta.

2. Next start making the sauce: melt the butter in a small saucepan then add the onion, cover and cook gently for 10 minutes, until tender but not brown. Stir in the garlic, cook for 1–2 minutes, then stir in the cream. Let the mixture simmer gently for about 10 minutes, until the cream has reduced a bit and thickened, then season well with salt and pepper.

3. When the water boils, add the pasta to the pan, then let it bubble away, uncovered, for about 8 minutes or until it is al dente.

4. Drain the pasta, return it to the still-warm saucepan and season with some salt, then add the sauce and most of the walnuts and stir so that all the pasta gets coated. Serve out on to warm plates with the remaining nuts sprinkled on top.

Wild Mushrooms in Cream with Potato and Celeriac Mash

If you're lucky enough to have some truly wild mushrooms, this is a wonderful way to cook them, but you can also improvise: sometimes you can buy bags of 'wild' mushrooms, or you can put together an assortment of different types of mushrooms from the supermarket: oyster mushrooms, brown chestnut mushrooms, shiitake, enokitake (the tiny white ones that come in clumps). I recommend using an all-butter ready-rolled puff pastry for the leaves; you won't need the whole quantity, but you can keep the rest for another recipe. For a simpler version of this recipe, serve the mushrooms with crisp, hot, buttery garlic bread instead of the puff pastry leaves, and a green salad.

Serves 4

40g (1½oz) butter

1kg (2lb 2oz) wild mushrooms, washed, trimmed and sliced as necessary, patted dry on kitchen paper

3 garlic cloves, crushed

1 tsp cornflour

120ml (4½fl oz) double cream

1 lemon, halved

Pinch of cayenne pepper

Salt and black pepper

Chopped flat-leaf parsley

For the mash

750g (1lb 10oz) potatoes, peeled and cut into even-size pieces

350g (12oz) celeriac, peeled and cut into even-size pieces

25g (1oz) butter

3–4 tbsp double cream

For the puff pastry leaves

1 packet ready-rolled all-butter puff pastry

1. Preheat the oven to 200ºC (400ºF), Gas 6.

2. Start with the mash: put the potatoes and celeriac into a large saucepan with water just to cover. Bring to the boil, then cover and leave to simmer until tender: 15–20 minutes.

3. Meanwhile, for the mushrooms, melt the butter in a large saucepan and add the mushrooms and garlic. Cook over a moderate heat, uncovered, for about 5–10 minutes, until they are tender, but if they produce a great deal of liquid, see tip overleaf.

4. Cut the puff pastry into leaf shapes, or circles, whatever you fancy. Put them on a baking sheet and bake according to the directions on the packet, until they are puffed up and golden.

5. When the potatoes and celeriac are ready, drain them, keeping the water, and mash thoroughly, either by hand or by passing them through a potato ricer back into the still-hot saucepan. Beating with a wooden spoon, mix in the butter, a little of the reserved cooking water, and enough cream to make a completely smooth, creamy, light mixture. Season with salt and pepper.

6. Quickly finish the mushrooms: scatter the cornflour over the top, pour in the cream and stir over the heat until the mixture boils and thickens. Remove from the heat, add a squeeze of lemon juice and some cayenne, salt and pepper to season.

continues overleaf

7. Serve the mushrooms, sprinkled with a little chopped parsley, with the puff pastry leaves and the potato and celeriac mash.

Tip: Sometimes mushrooms produce a lot of liquid as they cook. If this happens, either keep on cooking them for up to 20 minutes until the liquid has boiled away, or drain them, keeping the liquid as stock for another recipe, and start again with a clean pan and more butter.

Make it vegan: Use olive oil instead of butter (3 tbsp for the mushrooms, 2 tbsp for the mash), soya cream instead of dairy cream, and puff pastry made with vegetable fat.

Pappardelle with Wild Mushrooms

Lovely wide silky strips of pasta that you can really get your teeth into with delectable wild mushrooms: bliss on a plate! Wild mushrooms are quite easy to find in supermarkets these days; sometimes you can buy packs of them, or you can make up your own assortment, including some chestnut mushrooms, or some dried morels or porcini to make up the quantity as necessary. If you're using the dried mushrooms, prepare them according to the packet instructions before adding them to the rest.

Serves 4

3 tbsp olive oil

About 400g (14oz) wild mushrooms, trimmed, wiped and sliced as necessary

1 garlic clove, finely chopped

400g (14oz) pappardelle

Good knob of butter

Small bunch chopped flat-leaf parsley

Salt and black pepper

Freshly grated Parmesan-style cheese, to serve (optional)

1. Heat the olive oil in a large saucepan, add the mushrooms and fry, uncovered, for about 5 minutes, until tender, stirring from time to time. Add the garlic, and season with salt and black pepper.

2. Meanwhile, cook the pasta in plenty of boiling water until al dente. Drain the pasta, leaving a little water clinging to it, and return it to the pan, over a gentle heat. Add the mushrooms, butter and parsley, and toss lightly, until the butter has melted and the mixture is piping hot. Check the seasoning. Serve with grated Parmesan-style cheese at the table, if liked.

Make it vegan: Swirl a little extra olive oil into the pasta instead of the butter before serving, and leave out the cheese.

Wild Mushroom Risotto

The wild mushrooms in this are the dried porcini that are easy to find in supermarkets, and really give this risotto an intense mushroom flavour. For the rest, choose chestnut mushrooms if you can get them, because they have plenty of flavour, retain their firm texture and don't produce much liquid.

Serves 4

10g packet porcini mushrooms

1 bay leaf

1.5 litres (2½ pints) boiling water

1 tsp vegetable stock powder

3 tbsp olive oil

50g (2oz) butter

1 onion, chopped

350g (12oz) chestnut mushrooms

2 garlic cloves, crushed

350g (12oz) risotto rice

Salt and black pepper

Flat-leaf parsley, chopped

50g (2oz) fresh Parmesan-style cheese, cut into thin slivers

1. Put the porcini into a saucepan with the bay leaf, boiling water and stock powder. Simmer very gently over a low heat while you prepare the other ingredients.

2. Heat the olive oil and half the butter in a large saucepan, then add the onion, cover and cook for about 5 minutes, until soft but not browned.

3. Add the chestnut mushrooms to the onion with the garlic and rice. Stir for 2–3 minutes, until the rice is coated with the buttery juices.

4. Add a ladleful of the simmering water from the pan containing the porcini and stir well; once it has been absorbed, add another. Keep the water in the porcini pan simmering away and continue to add it to the risotto a ladleful at a time as each addition is absorbed, stirring the risotto constantly.

5. Using a slotted spoon, remove the porcini from the pan, chop them up and add them to the risotto. Stop adding water once the rice is tender but not soggy – al dente, in fact. This will be after about 20 minutes and you will probably have used all the water.

6. Stir in the rest of the butter and season to taste with salt and pepper. Serve immediately, scattered with the parsley and slivers of Parmesan-style cheese.

Griddled Courgette and Red Pepper Rice Bowls

I got the idea for this from the rice bowls they serve in the Fresh restaurants in Toronto: rice topped with all kinds of wonderful ingredients, tasty dressings and garnishes. Here, homemade hummus, chunky griddled slices of courgette, charred but still crunchy, and pieces of grilled red pepper are piled up on top of brown basmati rice and drizzled with soy ginger dressing, garlicky sunflower cream and scattered with toasted sunflower seeds and coriander leaves to make a very satisfying meal. You can vary this formula endlessly with different vegetables, sauces and garnishes.

Serves 4

Vegan

400g (14oz) brown basmati rice, rinsed

1 litre (1¾ pints) water

2 red peppers, deseeded

4 fat courgettes, each about 225g (8oz), sliced on the diagonal into pieces about 1cm (½in) thick at the widest part

Olive oil

Hummus (see page 59)

4 tbsp sunflower seeds, toasted, to serve

Leaves from a small bunch of fresh coriander, to serve

For the ginger soy drizzle

1 tbsp finely grated fresh ginger

3 tbsp toasted sesame oil

4 tbsp shoyu soy sauce

4 tbsp water

4 tbsp lemon juice

1. Put the rice and water into a saucepan, bring to the boil, then cover, turn down the heat and leave to cook gently for 25 minutes, or until all the water has been absorbed and the rice is tender.

2. Cut each pepper into about 8 flat pieces with a few extra odd-shaped trimmings. Place the pieces of pepper, shiny side up, in a single layer on a grill pan and put under a hot grill for about 10 minutes, or until they're browned in places and firm. Set aside.

3. Heat a griddle; brush the courgette slices lightly on both sides with olive oil. When the griddle is really hot, put some of the courgette slices on it. Leave them in place for 3–4 minutes, or until they are striped deep brown, then turn them over. When they're done, set aside, or keep warm under a grill, while you do the rest.

4. While the courgette slices are cooking, you can make the hummus (as on page 59) and sauces.

5. For the ginger soy drizzle, put all the ingredients into a small pan, bring to the boil, simmer for 4–5 minutes, then take off the heat and set aside.

ingredients and method continue overleaf

For the sunflower cream

100g (3½oz) sunflower seeds (raw, not toasted)

1 garlic clove, crushed

3 tbsp freshly squeezed lemon juice

200–250ml (7–9fl oz) water

Salt

6. For the sunflower cream, put the sunflower seeds, garlic, lemon juice and water into a blender (or use a hand-held blender) and blend to a smooth cream; the more powerful the blender, the more smooth and creamy the result. Season with salt to taste.

7. Divide the cooked rice between 4 plates. In the centre of the rice, pile the courgette slices, red pepper and hummus. Then pour over some of the ginger soy drizzle and the sunflower cream and scatter with the toasted sunflower seeds and some fresh coriander leaves. Or just let everyone help themselves!

Almond and Pecan Roast with Sherry Gravy

I invented this recipe in response to a reader's request for 'a nut roast that I can whizz up in the food processor and make in 30 minutes'. There's even time to cook Bircher Potatoes, page 188, and some Brussels Sprouts with Mustard-Maple Glaze and Sichuan Pepper, page 175, if you get really organised. You'll work hard, but it will be worth it!

Serves 4

Vegan

100g (3½oz) pecans
100g (3½oz) almonds
100g (3½oz) wholemeal bread
1 medium onion, cut into chunks
1 celery stick, roughly chopped
1 medium carrot, scraped and
    roughly chopped
2 garlic cloves, peeled
2 tsp dried mixed herbs
4 tsp shoyu soy sauce
2 tbsp olive oil
2 tbsp dried breadcrumbs
Salt and black pepper

For the sherry gravy

600ml (1 pint) water
1 tsp vegetable stock powder
3 tbsp shoyu soy sauce
1½ tbsp redcurrant jelly
1 tbsp cornflour
1½ tbsp freshly squeezed
    orange juice
1½ tbsp sherry

1. Preheat the oven to 180°C (350°F), Gas 4. Put a roasting tin into the oven to heat up.

2. Put the nut roast ingredients up to (and including) the shoyu soy sauce into a food processor and process to a pâté-like consistency. Season with a little salt.

3. Pour the olive oil into the roasting tin and put the tin back into the oven.

4. Scatter the dried breadcrumbs on to a board and put the nut mixture on top. Shape it into a brick shape, about 5cm (2in) high, and roll it in the crumbs to cover it all over.

5. Put the nut loaf into the roasting tin and turn it in the oil, so that it is coated all over.

6. Bake the nut roast for about 25 minutes, until it is golden brown and crisp, turning it after 10 minutes, and then again as it cooks, so that it browns evenly. While the roast is cooking, make the gravy.

7. Bring the water, stock powder, soy sauce and redcurrant jelly to the boil in a saucepan. Blend the cornflour with the orange juice and sherry. Stir a little of the hot liquid into the cornflour mixture, then tip this into the saucepan. Stir well, then simmer over a gentle heat until slightly thickened.

8. Serve the nut roast in slices with gravy, Bircher Potatoes, which you can cook in the oven at the same time as the roast, and some green vegetables.

Orange-scented Bulgur Pilaf

Pretty colours, summery flavours ... this is lovely as a light lunch with a crisp, leafy salad – I like to scoop it up with crunchy little gem lettuce leaves. When you slice the fennel, cut the bulb down as if you are cutting it into quarters or eighths, but try to make more pieces than that, as thin as you can, whilst keeping each still attached at the base: they need to be thin to cook in time.

Serves 4

Vegan

2 red onions, sliced into rings

2 medium fennel, shaved down the sides to remove any tough fibres, then sliced downwards into slim pieces, still attached at the base

2 tbsp olive oil

300g (11oz) bulgur wheat

Zest of 2 oranges, grated or cut into slim strands using a zester

Juice of 2 oranges made up to 600ml (1 pint) with water

A handful (about 40g/1½oz) each of green olives and black (Kalamata) olives

Small handful (about 50g/2oz) toasted, salted almonds cut into strands

Salt and black pepper

A scattering of roughly chopped flat-leaf parsley

1. Sauté the onions and fennel in the oil for 10 minutes, until both are tender to the point of a knife. Stir in the bulgur, and the orange zest and juice.

2. Bring to the boil, then take off the heat and leave it to stand, covered, for 15 minutes, or until the bulgur wheat is fluffy and tender.

3. Stir in the olives and salted almonds; season to taste. Scatter with some roughly chopped flat-leaf parsley and serve.

Wonderful Rice Pilaf

This, to me, says 'celebration'. It's packed with crunchy golden nuts, spices, plump dried fruits, so there are a lot of ingredients, but it's very easy to make, and served in a big, shallow dish, or piled up on a flat plate, it makes a beautiful centrepiece. Serve it with a bowl of pomegranate raita and some beautiful salads and dips, and let everyone help themselves.

Serves 4–6

300g (11oz) white basmati rice, well rinsed

400ml (14fl oz) water

¼ tsp turmeric

2 tbsp olive oil

1 onion, sliced

125g (4½oz) flaked almonds

50g (2oz) pine nuts

3 garlic cloves, crushed

1 tbsp cumin seeds

25g (1oz) pumpkin seeds

25g (1oz) pistachio nuts

1 tbsp poppy seeds

50g (2oz) plump raisins

50g (2oz) dried cranberries

1 lemon, halved

3 tbsp roughly chopped fresh coriander

Salt and black pepper

For the pomegranate raita

Seeds from 1 pomegranate (see tip below)

300ml (11fl oz) plain natural yoghurt

1. Put the rice (still wet from rinsing – this is essential) into a heavy-based pan with the water and turmeric. Bring to the boil, put a lid on the pan, and reduce the heat to a low simmer. Set a timer for 14 minutes. When the time has elapsed, immediately take the pan off the heat, without removing the lid (this is important!), and let it stand for another 8 minutes, to steam in its own heat. This method, which I learnt from Nadine Abensur, results in perfectly dry rice, with every grain separate, every time, but you have to follow it precisely.

2. While the rice is cooking, heat the oil in a large saucepan, add the onion, cover and cook for 10 minutes, until softened but not browned. Add the flaked almonds and pine nuts and stir for about 5 minutes until they're golden brown and fragrant. Add the garlic, cumin, pumpkin seeds, pistachios, poppy seeds, raisins and dried cranberries; cook for 1–2 minutes, then set aside.

3. To make the pomegranate raita, combine the yoghurt with enough of the pomegranate seeds to make a bright, tangy mixture.

4. When the rice is done, stir it gently with a fork, then squeeze a little lemon juice in, which will immediately brighten the colour to a beautiful pale gold.

5. Mix the rice gently with the nut mixture, and season with salt and pepper. Pile on to a warmed serving dish, scatter with the chopped coriander, and serve with the raita in a bowl alongside.

Tip: To remove the seeds from the pomegranate easily, cut the pomegranate in half round its equator, then holding it cut-side down over a bowl, whack it with a wooden spoon: the seeds will tumble out.

Mediterranean Strudel

Dramatic, crunchy golden filo pastry filled with layers of cashew and baby mushrooms, roasted red pepper, spinach and goat's cheese – this is such a stunning centrepiece dish that I couldn't leave it out of the book, although I admit it is a feat to get it done in 30 minutes. The best way to shape the strudel, and get the layers nice and defined, is to layer it up in a loaf tin, then turn it out on top of the filo pastry, like making a sand pie at the beach … sounds a bit fiddly, but it's easy.

Serves 6–8

1 tbsp olive oil

300g (11oz) button mushrooms, rinsed, left whole, or halved, depending on size

450–500g (about 1lb) ready-washed baby leaf spinach

300g (11oz) cashew nuts

100g (3½oz) crustless white bread

100g (3½oz) Parmesan-style cheese, finely grated

2 large garlic cloves

1 tsp vegetable stock powder

4 tbsp water

4 red peppers, cut into thick, flat slices and grilled (see tip overleaf) or 285g jar char-grilled red peppers, drained

200g (7oz) strong firm white goat's cheese, sliced

7 sheets of filo pastry

3–4 tbsp rapeseed oil

Salt, black pepper and grated nutmeg

1. Preheat the oven to 190ºC (375ºF), Gas 5; have ready a 900g (2lb) loaf tin lined with a strip of baking parchment to cover the base and narrow sides.

2. Heat the olive oil in a saucepan, add the mushrooms and cook for 2–3 minutes, until just tender. Remove from the heat.

3. Cook the spinach in a pan, with a few drops of water, for about 2 minutes, until collapsed; or cook in a microwave according to the packet directions. Put into a colander under the cold tap to cool it quickly, then squeeze it with your hands to extract excess water. Season the spinach with salt, pepper and nutmeg.

4. To make the cashew nut mixture, put the cashew nuts and bread into a food processor and blend until fine, then add Parmesan-style cheese, garlic, stock powder and water, and blend again until combined. Then stir in the mushrooms: it will seem a lot for the amount of cashew mixture, but that's fine.

5. Put just over half of the cashew mixture into the base of the loaf tin and press down firmly. Next add half of the red peppers in a layer, followed by half the spinach, then all the goat's cheese, and the rest of the spinach. Top with the rest of the red peppers, then the remaining cashew mixture for a final layer. Press it down well.

continues overleaf

6. Brush a flat baking sheet with oil, for cooking the strudel. Spread 2 sheets of filo pastry out lengthways on the baking sheet with an slight overlap between them, and brush with a little oil. It doesn't matter if the pastry extends beyond the baking sheet because it will be rolled up around the filling. Then cover with 2 more sheets of overlapping filo, this time widthways, and again brush with oil. Place another 2 sheets on top in the same direction as the first pair, brush them with oil.

7. Now turn your stripy mixture out of the tin on top of the filo pastry. Fold up the sides and edges, so that your loaf is wrapped up in filo, pressing it all firmly together, then scrunch the remaining sheet of filo on top.

8. Brush with the remaining oil, put into the oven, and bake for 15–20 minutes, until heated through and golden brown and crisp. You may need to cover it loosely with foil after about 10 minutes so that the filo doesn't get too brown before the inside is hot.

9. Let it cool for a few minutes before serving, then gently cut into thick slices with a sharp serrated knife, and serve.

Tip: If you're grilling your own peppers, cut each one into four roughly flat pieces, with a few extra odd-shaped trimmings. Place all the pieces of pepper in a single layer on a baking sheet or grill pan – you may need to do them in two batches – and put under a hot grill for about 10 minutes, or until they're browned in places and firm. If you want to peel off the papery skin once they're cold, that's up to you, but I generally just take off the very black bits that lift off easily.

Fast Falafel

I can't claim these are made in the authentic way with raw chickpeas – there are limits to what you can do in 30 minutes, after all – but I can promise you they're easy to make, taste wonderful, and appeal to all age groups ... They're great with the Middle Eastern Salad Platter (see page 158) and are also good stuffed into warm pitta bread with some chopped lettuce, tomato, cucumber and grated carrot; maybe a few black olives, too. For the spicing, try with a tablespoon each of cumin and coriander to begin with, then taste and see if you'd like to add more. For me, the spicier the better.

Serves 4

Vegan

125g (4½oz) millet

300ml (11fl oz) water

400g tin chickpeas, drained

1–2 tbsp ground cumin

1–2 tbsp ground coriander

2 spring onions, finely chopped

4 tbsp chopped fresh coriander

1 lemon, halved

1 tbsp freshly squeezed lemon juice

Salt and black pepper

1–2 tbsp wholemeal flour, to dust

Rapeseed oil, for frying

1. Put the millet into a pan with the water, bring to the boil, cover and cook for 15–20 minutes, until all the water has been absorbed and the millet is light and fluffy.

2. When the millet is done, put it with the chickpeas, cumin, ground coriander, spring onions, fresh coriander and a squeeze of fresh lemon into a food processor, and blend to a thick, sticky consistency. Taste and increase the spices as necessary, and season with salt and pepper.

3. Form the mixture into small balls and dust with a little flour (to help the shaping process).

4. Deep- or shallow-fry in rapeseed oil until golden brown, crisp and crunchy all over. Blot them on kitchen paper, and serve.

Middle Eastern Salad Platter with Baba Ganoosh

I love the way salad is served in Turkey – market-fresh vegetables with the minimum of preparation, on a large platter – especially when it's served with baba ganoosh, that gorgeous smooth, smoky, garlicky, slightly bitter dip … the dip isn't difficult to make at home as long as you have some way of charring the aubergine. I put it on an old oven rack over a burner on my gas cooker and it takes 10–15 minutes. You could put it under a hot grill, but it might take a bit longer to get fully charred and tender. Otherwise, homemade hummus goes very well too (see page 59). This salad is the ideal accompaniment for the Fast Falafel (see page157).

Serves 4

Vegan

Bunch of spring onions,
    lightly trimmed

Bunch of radishes, leaves
    still attached

4 carrots, scrubbed, cut into batons

½ cucumber or 2 Middle Eastern
    cucumbers, cut into batons

Sprigs of flat-leaf parsley

4 tomatoes, quartered

125g (4½oz) chillies preserved
    in brine, drained

Lemon wedges, to garnish

For the baba ganoosh

1 medium aubergine

1 large garlic clove, peeled

2 tbsp freshly squeezed lemon juice

3 tbsp tahini

1–2 tbsp olive oil (optional)

Sea salt

1 tbsp roughly chopped
    flat-leaf parsley

1. Start with the baba ganoosh: char the whole aubergine, as described above: it's a good idea to keep the stem still attached, because you can use this to turn and move the aubergine: kitchen tongs are useful here, too. Move the aubergine around over the burner (or under the grill) until it's more or less charred all over, and tender, then cool it quickly under the cold tap and remove the stem. Pull off the charred skin, but there's no need to be too fussy about this. A little left behind adds nicely to the smoky flavour.

2. Put the aubergine into a food processor (or deep container if you use a hand-blender) along with the garlic, lemon juice and tahini, and blend until really smooth. Season with salt. You could add the olive oil, which is a traditional ingredient for this dip, at this point, but I don't always add it at all, or sometimes I just drizzle it over the top of the dip, so have a taste first and make up your own mind. Put the dip into a small bowl and scatter the parsley on top.

3. To make the salad, arrange everything in colourful heaps on a large plate, with the bowl of baba ganoosh in the centre, and garnish with lemon wedges.

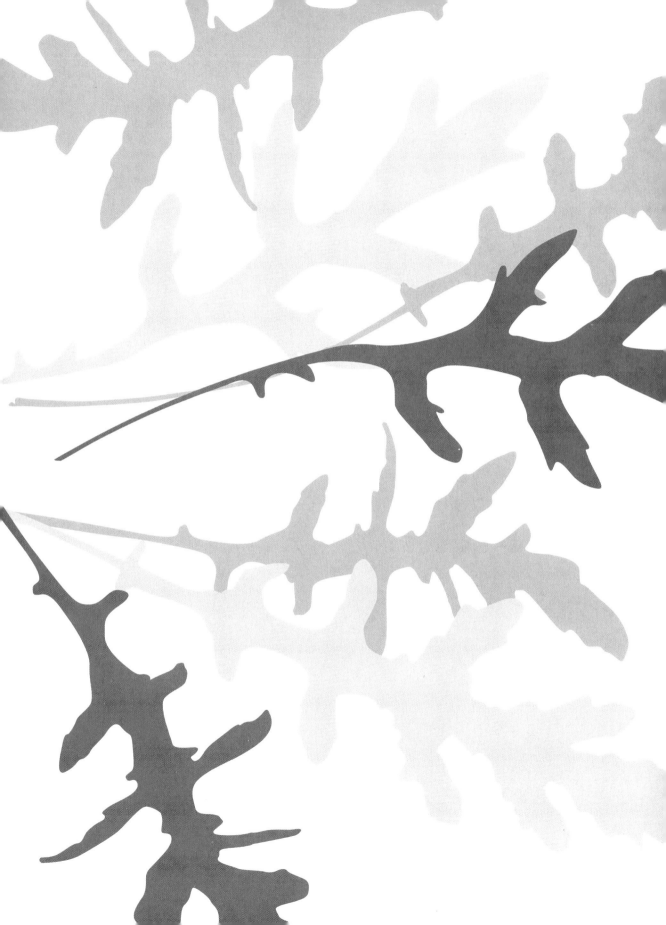

Salads & Sides

Summer Salad of Beans and Herbs

This, for me, is one of those summer-on-a-plate dishes. It's so easy and refreshing, perfect on a hot summer's day, either as a light meal in itself or as a side dish, or supplemented with some good bread and salad leaves, fragrant tomatoes, a creamy dip, a bowl of olives – to make an easy spread. These quantities are right for a main dish for two people, or a side dish for four; it's easy to multiply up and is a good buffet party dish.

Serves 2–4

Vegan

250g (9oz) thin green beans, trimmed as much or as little as you like

400g tin cannellini beans, drained and rinsed

4 spring onions, thinly sliced

1 heaped tbsp chopped flat-leaf parsley

1 tbsp chopped chives

1 tbsp chopped mint or dill

For the dressing

2 tbsp cider vinegar

1 tbsp olive oil

Salt and black pepper

1. Cook the beans in 1cm (½in) boiling water until tender and bright green: 4–6 minutes, depending on their size, but make sure you get them tender, not 'squeaky' when you bite them. Drain into a colander and refresh under cold water.

2. Meanwhile, put the cannellini beans into a salad bowl with the spring onions, parsley, chives and mint or dill.

3. Add the cooked beans, still warm, to the bowl and drizzle over the vinegar and olive oil. Mix gently, and season with salt and black pepper.

Baby Spinach, Apple, Celery and Hazelnut Salad

This is a very pleasing mixture, with lots of contrasting colours, textures and flavours. I think it makes a lovely autumn or winter salad; you could serve it simply with a baked potato, or marry it up with Gratin Dauphinoise, page 137, for a special lunch or light supper.

Serves 4

Vegan

80g (3oz) hazelnuts

4 sweet English apples, such as Russets or Cox, peeled and sliced

1 celery heart, sliced

200g (7oz) baby leaf spinach

2 small/medium spring onions, chopped

For the dressing

2 tbsp cider vinegar

2 tbsp olive oil

1–2 tsp maple syrup

½ tsp Dijon mustard

¼–½ tsp sea salt

1. If the hazelnuts are not already skinned and toasted, spread them out in a dry roasting tin and bake in a moderate oven – 180°C (350°F), Gas 4 – for 5–10 minutes, or until golden brown beneath the brown outer layer. Tip on to a plate and leave to cool, then rub them in a clean tea towel to remove most of the brown skins. Set aside.

2. To make the salad, put the apples, celery, spinach and spring onions into a bowl.

3. Make a dressing by whisking, or shaking, all the ingredients together, sweetening it and salting it to taste.

4. Just before the meal, pour the dressing into the bowl, add the hazelnuts, and gently toss the salad.

Salad of Chicory, Fresh Dill, Wild Rocket and Avocado

This is quick, pretty to look at and delicious. Be generous with the dill and rocket: they're part of the salad rather than a garnish.

Serves 4

Vegan

3 chicory, leaves separated

6–8 good sprigs of dill, roughly chopped

4 handfuls of wild rocket

1 large or 2 small ripe avocados

For the dressing

1–2 garlic cloves

4 tbsp olive oil

Juice of 1 lemon

Dash of balsamic vinegar

Salt and black pepper

1. Put the chicory, dill and rocket into a salad bowl.

2. Peel, stone and slice the avocados and add them to the bowl.

3. Make a dressing by crushing the garlic and mixing it to a paste with a little salt, then blending it with the olive oil, lemon juice and a dash of balsamic vinegar. Check the seasoning and add a little more salt, and some pepper, as necessary.

4. Add the dressing to the salad bowl, toss the leaves gently, and serve.

Red Cabbage Casserole

This is one of my favourite vegetable dishes: it's easy to make, is delicious on its own or with some plain rice or mashed or jacket potato, but it also goes well with so many dishes and provides a natural gravy for the meal. This recipe makes quite a lot, but it reheats beautifully and if anything is even better next day. It's even good cold. It's worth taking the trouble to shred the cabbage quite finely because then it will cook more quickly.

Serves 4–6

Vegan

1 small red cabbage, about 750g (1lb 10oz), finely shredded

1 large apple, cored and diced

2 handfuls of sultanas

500ml (18fl oz) apple juice

2 tbsp cider vinegar (see tip below)

1. Put the cabbage, apple, sultanas, apple juice and cider vinegar into a large saucepan.

2. Bring to the boil, then cover and leave to cook gently for 25 minutes, or until the cabbage is really tender, stirring once or twice during cooking.

3. Check the seasoning, and serve.

Tip: You can use ume seasoning instead of, or as well as, cider vinegar. A little added to red cabbage intensifies the colour as well as the flavour. It's very salty; you only need a teaspoonful or so.

Easy Crunchy Coleslaw

Homemade coleslaw is so quick and easy to make, and so much better than anything the shops sell, that I just can't understand why anyone ever buys it. The perfect cabbages to use for this are the little green pointed ones that you can buy all the year round; and bought mayonnaise is perfectly OK to use for the dressing. I particularly like this with crunchy golden Bircher Potatoes, page 188, for a very quick and satisfying meal, perfect for a quick Saturday lunch for the family. Leftover slaw keeps perfectly in the fridge for at least 24 hours.

Serves 4

½ pointed pale green cabbage, about 350–400g (12–14oz), core discarded

1 large carrot, grated

1 small onion, finely chopped

4 heaped tbsp mayonnaise, or half mayonnaise, half plain yoghurt

2 tbsp freshly squeezed lemon juice

Salt and black pepper

1. Shred the cabbage finely, either using the shredding attachment to a food processor, or by cutting it on a firm chopping board with a sharp knife.

2. Put the shredded cabbage into a bowl along with the carrot, onion, mayonnaise, lemon juice, and salt and pepper to taste and mix well.

3. You can serve it straight away, or let it stand for a while, in which case the cabbage will be a bit softer.

Tips: This is also delicious made with vinaigrette instead of mayonnaise.

Try adding any of the following: finely chopped red or gold peppers; chopped chives, spring onions or parsley; chopped walnuts, sunflower or pumpkin seeds – add these just before serving; plump raisins or sultanas; chopped fresh or canned pineapple or sweetcorn; chopped celery.

Make it vegan: Either make the salad with vinaigrette, use a non-dairy mayo, such as the delicious Tofu Mayonnaise on page 26 or vegan garlic mayo available from health shops.

Shaved Kohlrabi Salad with Watercress

If they had vegetables on Mars, they'd look like kohlrabi … I love the delicate flavour of this pale green vegetable, with its stems coming out at odd angles, but I think the most interesting and pleasing thing about it is its crisp, crunchy texture, which this recipe shows off to good advantage. This is a light, clean salad, perfect for serving with a rich main course, as well as eating on its own.

Serves 4

Vegan

2–3 kohlrabi

Bunch or packet of watercress, trimmed

Juice of ½ lemon

2 tbsp olive oil

Sea salt and black pepper

1. Cut the stems off the kohlrabi then peel it lightly, as near the surface as you can.

2. Slice the kohlrabi into paper-thin rounds, using a sharp knife and a steady hand, or a mandolin. You can keep the rounds whole, or cut them into half moons if you prefer, depending on the original size of the kohlrabi.

3. Put the kohlrabi and watercress on a shallow serving dish.

4. Mix the lemon juice with the olive oil and a little salt; drizzle this over the top of the kohlrabi, then grind some black pepper coarsely over the top.

Tip: Although it does make a welcome appearance in organic vegetable boxes, kohlrabi is not as easy to find as I'd like, so make sure you grab it when you can.

Braised Carrots with Cumin

Although I like most vegetables on the crunchy side, when it comes to braised carrots, I prefer them to be tender, soft as butter and sweet as candy: just like these, in fact. If you prefer them a bit more al dente, just stop cooking them when they reach the degree of tenderness you like. This is lovely made with baby carrots, just scrubbed, with the leaves cut but some of the stem still attached; but it also works perfectly with older carrots, scrubbed, or peeled if not organic, and cut into batons the size of your little finger.

Serves 4

Vegan

750g (1lb 10oz) carrots, prepared as described in the introduction

4 tbsp olive oil

4 garlic cloves, sliced

1 tsp ground cumin

1 tsp whole cumin seeds

Juice of ½ lemon

150ml (5fl oz) water

Salt and black pepper

1–2 tbsp chopped flat-leaf parsley, to serve

1. Put the carrots into a saucepan with the olive oil, garlic, ground and whole cumin seeds, lemon juice, water, and some salt and pepper. Bring to the boil, then cover and cook gently for about 30 minutes, checking occasionally to make sure they're not sticking.

2. They're done when they feel very tender to the point of a knife, and the water has reduced to a syrupy golden glaze. Scatter with chopped fresh parsley.

Carrot Salad with Coriander and Orange

I like the simplicity and clean freshness of this salad, but for a richer mixture, you could use vinaigrette to dress the carrot, or stir in 1–2 tbsp olive oil.

Serves 4

Vegan

400g (14oz) carrots, grated

Small bunch of coriander, chopped

4 spring onions, chopped

Juice of 1 orange, or ½ lemon

Salt

1. Mix all the ingredients together and season to taste.

Purple Sprouting Broccoli with Gomasio

If the broccoli is perfect, it needs little adornment: a sprinkling of ume, if you like, a squeeze of lemon or lime juice, a little drizzle of toasted sesame oil if you're going to serve it with an oriental type of dish, or olive oil for a Mediterranean one; and, to top it all, a sprinkling of delicious nutty-tasting gomasio, sesame salt.

Serves 4

Vegan

400g (14oz) purple sprouting
  (or Tenderstem-type) broccoli
  (see tip below)

1 tbsp freshly squeezed lemon
  or lime juice

1 tbsp toasted sesame or olive oil

1–2 tsp ume seasoning
  (see tip on page 84, optional)

1–2 tsp gomasio (see page 179)

1. Put the broccoli into a saucepan with 6 tablespoons of water. Bring to the boil, cover and cook gently until you can pierce the stems with the point of a knife: 5–15 minutes, depending on the heat, and the thickness of the stems. Keep an eye on the water and top up with a little boiling water if necessary. By the time the broccoli is cooked, all the water may have gone; if not, drain off any that remains.

2. Toss the broccoli with the lemon or lime juice, drizzle with the oil and ume seasoning, if you're using this, sprinkle with gomasio, and serve.

Tip: To get the most out of purple sprouting broccoli – or the green 'Tenderstem-type' – it's worth taking time with the preparation: run a swivel-blade potato peeler down the stems, all round, to remove any tough woodiness, and to make the stems thinner so they cook in the same amount of time as the tender heads. I also like to use as little water to cook them in as I can possibly get away with, so that all the nutrients and flavour are conserved and none gets thrown down the sink. You do have to keep your eye on the pan, though, if you do this, and watch the level of the heat and the water, adding a bit more boiling water if necessary.

Red Chard with Olive Oil and Lemon

To get the most out of red chard, you need to cook the stems and the leaves for differing lengths of time, as in this recipe. This is one of my favourite vegetables.

Serves 4

Vegan

1kg (2lb 2oz) red chard

Salt and black pepper

Lemon wedges, to serve

Olive oil, to serve

1. Separate the stems of the chard from the leaves; cut the stems into 2–4cm (1–2in) lengths and chop the leaves roughly.

2. Bring 1cm (½in) water to the boil in a large saucepan; add the chard stems, cover and cook for 2–3 minutes, until the stems are beginning to soften.

3. Add the chard leaves to the pan, on top of the stems. Cover and cook until both stems and leaves are tender: this could be anything from 2–4 minutes, depending on how tender they were to start with.

4. Drain as necessary, and serve the perfectly cooked chard and stems on warm plates, offering salt, pepper, lemon wedges and olive oil for people to dress it themselves.

Brussels Sprouts with Mustard-maple Glaze and Sichuan Pepper

My main tip for cooking perfect Brussels is one I learnt from my mother: cut them in half, then they cook perfectly without any sogginess. If you then toss them in a sweet maple-mustard glaze, to balance their slight bitterness, and finish them off with a generous sprinkling of pepper – Sichuan peppercorns if you want to be a bit exotic, but ordinary black ones are also fine – you'll end up with a dish that everyone loves!

Serves 4–6

Vegan

400g (14oz) trimmed
 Brussels sprouts

For the sweet mustard glaze

2 tsp Dijon mustard

3 tbsp maple syrup

For the pepper

1 tsp Sichuan peppercorns

1 tsp sea salt

1. Cut the Brussels sprouts in half from the top to the stalk end.

2. Bring 1cm (½in) water to the boil in a saucepan, put in the sprouts, bring back to the boil, cover with a lid, and cook until the sprouts are just tender: maybe 4–5 minutes, maybe a shade longer, but don't let them get anywhere near sogginess. Drain immediately.

3. While the sprouts are cooking, make the glaze: put the mustard into a small bowl and gradually add the maple syrup, stirring all the time. Set aside.

4. For the pepper, put the Sichuan peppercorns into a small saucepan and stir over a moderate heat for a few seconds until they smell aromatic. Tip them straight out of the pan to prevent further cooking. Grind them in a pestle and mortar with the salt.

5. Toss the Brussels sprouts in the mustard glaze, so they're glistening and shiny, sprinkle with the ground Sichuan peppercorn and salt mixture, and serve.

Tip: The Sichuan peppercorn-salt mix is nice sprinkled over other cooked vegetables – try it on green beans, carrots and cabbage – and also rice; in fact, once you get the taste for it, you'll be sprinkling it over everything for a while!

Asian Flavours Salad

A simple herb salad with a refreshing lime dressing.

Serves 4

½ pointed pale green cabbage

4 spring onions

Small bunch each of coriander,
    basil and mint

For the dressing

Juice of 1 lime

2 tbsp olive oil

1 garlic clove, crushed

Salt, pepper and clear honey
    or sugar to taste

1. Put the cabbage, cut-side down, on a large board, and using a sharp knife cut it across into thin shreds, cutting out and discarding the core. Put the shredded cabbage into a large bowl.

2. Trim and chop the spring onions, coriander, basil and mint, and add to the bowl.

3. Make the dressing straight into the bowl: add the lime juice, olive oil and garlic, and gently toss, making sure the garlic is well distributed.

4. Season to taste with salt, pepper and sugar or honey. Serve the salad in a pretty bowl.

Make it vegan: Use the sugar option in the dressing instead of honey.

Asian Pressed Salad with Gomasio

Asian pressed salads are very quick and easy to make: you shred or slice your vegetables, sprinkle with a little salt, top with a plate and a weight and leave them for 20–30 minutes. This softens the vegetables, rather as a dressing would, but without any added oil, so the result is light and refreshing. A pretty garnish is a sprinkling of gomasio; this is a tasty condiment that goes very well with many Asian dishes. It will keep for up to 14 days in a jar in the fridge, though it's nicest when made fresh.

Serves 4

1 round lettuce or Batavia, shredded

Bunch or packet (100g) radishes, trimmed and sliced into rounds

A small bunch of dill – or could use any other pretty herb, to tone in with the dish with which this is to be served

1 tsp sea salt

For the gomasio

1 tsp sea salt

3–4 tbsp sesame seeds

1. Put the lettuce, radishes and dill into a colander set over a bowl and sprinkle with salt.

2. Gently massage the salad with clean hands, rubbing the salt into the ingredients.

3. Top the salad with a plate and a weight, such as some cans or a litre container of water, and leave for at least 20–25 minutes. Discard any liquid the vegetables produce.

4. To make the gomasio, put the salt into a dry saucepan and stir over the heat for a few seconds, to remove any moisture, then add the sesame seeds. Stir over a moderate heat for 3–4 minutes, until the seeds start to smell toasty, change colour slightly and jump about in the pan. Remove from the heat and immediately tip into a bowl, to prevent the seeds from becoming too brown. Grind to a coarse powder in an electric coffee grinder or with a pestle and mortar: a Japanese ridged one, a suribachi, is traditionally used, but a normal one is fine.

5. Put the salad into a pretty bowl or serving plates and sprinkle with the gomasio.

Tip: You can vary the vegetables; if you're using harder ones like cabbage, celery or carrots, allow a bit longer – an hour or so for them to soften. These will keep well in the fridge for up to 24 hours.

Roasted Cauliflower Platter

This delicious and very pretty platter gives cauliflower the respect it deserves and makes it the star of the show.

Serves 4

Vegan

1 medium cauliflower, trimmed and cut down into thick slices (like slicing a loaf of bread)

Olive oil

1. Preheat the oven to 190°C (375°F), Gas 5.

2. Brush the cauliflower slices with olive oil and place in a baking tin. Roast for 25 minutes, or until tender and lightly browned and a bit crisp, turning them after about 15 minutes.

3. Make a pretty platter with the cauliflower slices. To make as part of a meal, serve with the French-style Petit Pois (on page 181), Asian Pressed Salad (on page 179) and a big spoonful of hummus (see page 59) in the centre.

Mixed Heirloom Tomato Salad

If you're lucky enough to find, or clever enough to grow, some heirloom tomatoes, make them into this wonderful salad: surely the queen of summer salads!

Serves 4

Vegan

900g mixed heirloom tomatoes, as many colours, shapes and sizes as you can find: big, small, green, red, yellow, stripy – whatever are available

2–3 tbsp extra virgin olive oil

Juice of ½ lemon

Sea salt and black pepper

2–3 sprigs of basil, to serve

1. Slice the tomatoes and put them into a bowl. Drizzle over the olive oil and lemon juice, sprinkle with some salt – crunchy sea salt if possible – and grind over some pepper.

2. Leave on one side for 20 minutes or so, then tear the basil leaves over the top and serve.

French-style Petit Pois

Unless you can get tender, just-picked peas, frozen ones are the best option. Cooking them in this classic French way makes them taste garden-fresh.

Serves 4
Vegan

1 tbsp olive oil

1 small onion, sliced

Lettuce leaves

Frozen peas, rinsed under the hot
    water tap if straight from
    the freezer

1. Heat the olive oil in a medium saucepan, add the onion, and let it cook gently without browning for 5 minutes. Add the lettuce, then the peas on top and a tablespoon of water. Cover and set over a gentle heat for 10 minutes or so until the lettuce has wilted and the peas are hot.

Chopped Multicoloured Salad

This is such a pretty salad, with contrasting colours and textures. It's particularly nice to serve when you want a light, refreshing accompaniment to a meal, or when you want a salad that will stay fresh for some time – for a buffet, for instance.

Serves 4
Vegan

1 little gem lettuce

60g (2½oz) red cabbage

Small bunch of flat-leaf parsley

1 celery heart

½ yellow pepper, deseeded

½ red pepper, deseeded

1 medium carrot

1 tomato

4 spring onions

For the dressing

1 tbsp cider vinegar

1 tbsp olive oil

Salt

1. Cut the lettuce leaves into 2cm (¾in) pieces. Cut the cabbage across into shreds, then cut these across, so you have small pieces; chop the parsley. Put them all into a bowl.

2. Cut the celery, peppers and carrot into matchsticks then across into tiny dice, and add to the bowl. Chop the tomato and spring onions, and add these too.

3. Add the cider vinegar and olive oil, and a dash of salt, to the bowl and toss the salad gently.

Radicchio with Raspberry Vinegar

The first time I made this, I used a wonderful raspberry vinegar I'd been given, with whole raspberries in it, and it was fantastic: it was, in fact, the inspiration for the recipe. By all means use vinegar like that if you can find it, but since then I've been using ordinary raspberry vinegar plus a handful of fresh or frozen raspberries, and it's perfect. This recipe also works beautifully with firm little gem lettuces if you can't find radicchio, though it gives quite a different result.

Serves 4

Vegan

1 large radicchio, quartered,
    or 2 smaller ones, halved

Wild rocket leaves, to serve

For the raspberry vinegar marinade

6 tbsp raspberry vinegar

Small handful fresh or frozen
    raspberries

Salt and black pepper

1. To make the marinade, mix all the ingredients together, crushing the raspberries a bit with the back of the spoon.

2. Put the chunks of radicchio into a shallow dish and cover with the marinade. Set aside until about 8 minutes before you want to serve it.

3. Remove the radicchio from the marinade, shaking any excess back into the dish. Put it under the grill, or on a fine mesh grid over a barbecue, the cut side towards the heat. Grill for about 3 minutes, or until the radicchio is beginning to wilt. If you're cooking it over a barbecue, turn it so that the cut side is uppermost, spoon any remaining marinade over, including any berries, and cook for 2–3 minutes more. If you're cooking it under the grill, there's no need to turn the radicchio – it's already cut-side up.

4. Serve at once: it's great on its own, as a side dish, but I rather like it served on top of some wild rocket leaves.

Tip: You could could drizzle a little olive oil over the top, before or after grilling, if you prefer.

Pan-fried Cabbage with Tomato Sauce

This is a lovely substantial vegetable dish: cabbage cut into big, satisfying wedges, browned in olive oil then braised with tomatoes until they are tender and bathed in a gorgeous tomato sauce.

Serves 4

Vegan

1 medium-sized pale green pointed cabbage, or Savoy cabbage with its tough outer leaves removed

2–3 tbsp olive oil

4 tomatoes, chopped

2 garlic cloves, crushed

2 tbsp sun-dried tomato paste

4 tbsp water

Salt and pepper

1. Cut the cabbage into four wedges. Heat the olive oil in a large, wide saucepan (or big frying pan with a lid). Put in the cabbage wedges, one cut-side down, and fry for 2–3 minutes until lightly browned, then turn them over – kitchen tongs are good for this – and brown the second cut side.

2. Add the tomatoes, garlic and the tomato paste to the pan, pushing them under the cabbage wedges so the cabbage is sitting on top of the tomato mixture. Pour in the water down the sides of the pan. Season with salt and pepper.

3. Bring to the boil, then cover and leave to cook gently for 20 minutes, or until the cabbage is meltingly tender and the tomatoes have collapsed into a thick sauce.

4. Check the seasoning of the sauce, then serve.

Baby Broad Beans in the Pod with Creamy Parsley Sauce

Broad beans are one of the vegetables I feel are best bought frozen rather than fresh (the other is petits pois), unless you can find very tender, young broad beans, not much thicker than your little finger. Then, if you're lucky enough to find these, the very best way to cook them is like French beans, pods and all, with a good old-fashioned parsley sauce.

Serves 4

500g (1lb 2oz) tender baby broad beans in their pods, trimmed as necessary, and left whole or cut into 5cm (2in) pieces

For the parsley sauce

25g (1oz) butter

1 rounded tbsp flour

400ml (14fl oz) milk: soya milk gives the creamiest result (buy unsweetened)

2 heaped tbsp chopped parsley

Salt, freshly ground pepper and nutmeg

1. Start with the sauce: put the butter, flour and milk into a saucepan and bring to the boil, whisking, until thick and smooth.

2. Let the sauce simmer gently for a few minutes to cook the flour. Remove from the heat, and season to taste with salt, pepper and nutmeg.

3. Cook the broad beans in a little boiling water, with a lid on the pan, for 5–6 minutes, or until tender; drain.

4. Reheat the sauce as necessary, then add to the beans, sprinkle in the parsley, and stir gently. Check the seasoning, and serve.

Crunchy Roast Parsnips with Horseradish Dip

Sweet crunchy roasted parsnips are irresistible, especially when served with a cool, tangy horseradish dip. Smallish, tender parsnips are best for this and I find that if you cut off the root end before it becomes thick, and then quarter the remaining parsnip, you end up with 'chips' that are reasonably uniform in size.

Serves 4

500g (1lb 2oz) parsnips, scrubbed, trimmed and cut into chunky chips

8 tbsp olive or rapeseed oil

50g (2oz) semolina

For the horseradish dip

150ml (5fl oz) crème fraîche or yoghurt

1 tbsp creamed horseradish or horseradish sauce

Salt and black pepper

1. Preheat oven to 230ºC (450ºF), Gas 8.

2. Cook the parsnips in 1cm (½in) boiling water for 8 minutes, until they are becoming tender.

3. Just before they're done, pour the oil in to a roasting tin and put into the oven to heat.

4. Drain the parsnips well and scatter with the semolina, turning them so they all get coated.

5. Put the parsnips into the oil (no need to turn them at this point) and bake until golden brown and crisp, turning them after about 10 minutes.

6. While the parsnips are cooking, make the dip by mixing the crème fraîche or yoghurt with the horseradish. Season to taste.

7. Remove the parsnips from the oven, blot on kitchen paper, then put on to a serving dish or individual plates. Serve with the horseradish dip.

Make it vegan: use non-dairy horseradish sauce for the dip or use Tofu Mayonnaise (see page 26) instead.

Bircher Potatoes

Invented by Dr Bircher Benner, who also created the original version of muesli, these have long been a favourite in my family, and are ideal for the quick cook because they can be baked in 30 minutes. The result is a cross between jacket and roast potatoes – or jacket potatoes with one side that is like a crunchy golden roast potato. This description doesn't do them justice: you'll just have to try them for yourself!

Serves 4

Vegan

8–12 smallish-medium
    potatoes, scrubbed

Olive oil

Crunchy sea salt

A sprinkling of caraway seeds
    (optional)

1. Preheat the oven to 200°C (400°F), Gas 6.

2. Cut the potatoes in half lengthways and put them, cut-side down, on a lightly oiled baking sheet. Sprinkle lightly with sea salt and with caraway seeds if you're using these.

3. Bake for about 25 minutes, or until the potatoes are tender on top and crisp and golden underneath.

Tip: Choose smallish (but not baby) potatoes – about 125g (4½oz) is right for this, so that they cook in 20–25 minutes, or larger ones, as for jacket baked potatoes, if time is no object. I like to use organic potatoes when I'm going to eat the skins.

Millet, Cauliflower and Parsley Mash

Millet and cauliflower are cooked separately then mashed together – you can use a food processor or hand-held blender for this – to make a creamy mixture that rather resembles mashed potatoes in taste and appearance. It's a classic recipe from the macrobiotic diet, in which potatoes are not generally eaten. I think it makes a pleasant change from potatoes, rice or couscous as the starch element of a meal, and the fact that it contains a healthy vegetable too is a bonus.

Serves 4

Vegan

225g (8oz) millet

400ml (14fl oz) water

1 medium cauliflower, trimmed and divided into florets

2 tbsp olive oil

Salt and black pepper

1. Put the millet into a dry pan and set over a medium heat for about 4 minutes, stirring often, until it smells toasted. Pour in the water, being careful because it will bubble up and produce steam. Bring back to the boil, cover and leave to cook for 15 minutes, or until it has absorbed all the water and looks fluffy and pale.

2. Meanwhile, bring 2.5cm (1in) water to the boil in a saucepan, add the cauliflower, cover with a lid and cook until tender, about 6–7 minutes, depending on the size of the florets. Drain well.

3. Purée the cauliflower and millet with the olive oil, using a food processor or hand-held blender, until smooth and creamy. Season with salt and black pepper. Reheat gently before serving.

Tip: Make any mash that's left over into cakes, dip in flour, and shallow fry until golden brown and crisp, just as you would leftover mashed potatoes.

Roast Potato Wedges with Sea Salt and Balsamic Vinegar

The best potatoes to use for these are Maris Piper potatoes; they come out crisp, crunchy and golden every time.

Serves 4

Vegan

4 large potatoes, scrubbed and cut into long slim wedges – maybe eighths – not more than 1cm (½in) at the thickest part

8 tbsp olive oil

50g (2oz) semolina

Sea salt

Balsamic vinegar

1. Preheat the oven to 230°C (450°F), Gas 8.

2. Parboil the potatoes in 1cm (½in) water for 5 minutes; 2 minutes before they're done, pour the olive oil into a large roasting tin and put into the oven to heat up.

3. Drain the potatoes thoroughly, then sprinkle with the semolina and move the potatoes around so that they are evenly coated.

4. Put the potatoes into the roasting tin and place in the oven.

5. Bake for 10–15 minutes, then turn the potatoes and bake for a further 5 minutes or so until the potatoes are golden and crunchy.

6. Turn the potatoes out on to a large plate or tin lined with kitchen paper to blot off any excess oil, then put them on to a serving platter and sprinkle with a scattering of sea salt and a drizzle of balsamic vinegar; or serve these separately for people to help themselves.

Sweet Things

Blueberry Crumble

Everyone loves crumble, don't they? For a fast, hot, satisfying pudding, I don't think this can be beaten.

Serves 4

250g (9oz) blueberries

1 tbsp cornflour

284g jar wild blueberry
    no-added-sugar jam (see page 201)

75g (3oz) rolled oats

75g (3oz) wholemeal spelt flour

4 tbsp cold-pressed
    golden rapeseed oil

5 tbsp demerara sugar

Pouring cream, or vanilla
    ice cream, to serve

1. Preheat the oven to 190°C (375°F), Gas 5.

2. Put the blueberries into a shallow ovenproof dish, sprinkle them with the cornflour, then add the jam and mix gently.

3. To make the quick crunchy topping, mix the rolled oats and spelt flour in a bowl. Use a fork to stir in the rapeseed oil and make a slightly lumpy, crumbly mixture, then lightly mix in 4 tablespoons of the demerara sugar.

4. Spoon the topping over the blueberries, scatter the remaining sugar over the top, and bake for 15–20 minutes, until the crumble is crunchy and golden brown and the fruit bubbling up around the edges. Serve with pouring cream or vanilla ice cream.

Make it vegan: Substitute soya cream or ice cream for the dairy versions, or simply serve the crumble on its own.

Blackberry and Apple Compote with Mascarpone and Toasted Hazelnuts

A classic combination that is always popular and especially wonderful if you've been able to pick the blackberries from the hedgerows yourself. I prefer to use sweet eating apples for this, rather than cooking apples, because that way you hardly have to add any sugar, though you could use cooking apples and sweeten them to taste if you prefer.

Serves 4

1kg (2lb 2oz) sweet eating apples, peeled, cored and sliced

2 tbsp water

No-sugar-added apricot jam (see page 201), honey or maple syrup, to taste

500g (1lb 2oz) blackberries

25g (1oz) toasted hazelnuts (see page 201)

Mascarpone cheese, to serve

1. Put the apples into a heavy based saucepan with the water. Cover and cook gently for 10–15 minutes, or until the apples are tender, checking from time to time to make sure they are not sticking.

2. Taste the mixture and sweeten with apricot jam, maple syrup or honey as necessary.

3. Put the blackberries into another saucepan, without any water, and cook them for a few minutes, until the juices run.

4. Gently fold the blackberries through the apple mixture. You can serve this straight away, or leave it until it's cold.

5. Scatter the hazelnuts over the top, and serve with mascarpone.

Rhubarb and Ginger Compote

Fresh-tasting and succulent, this is good served cold, warm or hot. If it is not to be a vegan dish you could serve it with almond- or orange-flavoured biscuits and some thick yoghurt or cream.

Serves 4

Vegan

2 pieces of stem ginger preserved in syrup

1kg (2lb 2oz) rhubarb

50g (2oz) sugar

4 tbsp ginger syrup from the jar

1. Finely chop the ginger. Trim the rhubarb and remove any stringy bits then cut it into 2.5cm (1in) lengths. Add the rhubarb pieces to the pan with the sugar, ginger syrup and chopped ginger, reserving some ginger for decoration.

2. Cover and leave to cook very gently for 2–3 minutes. Stir gently, then cook for a further 2–3 minutes, until the rhubarb is tender. Decorate with the reserved chopped ginger before serving.

Apricot Compote

This is a wonderful way to transform apricots that are too hard to eat raw. They look beautiful in a single layer on a shallow white dish: tender golden apricots glistening in a shiny glaze. If you like, you could stir the seeds from a vanilla pod into the glaze.

Serves 4

600–700g (1½lb) apricots

400ml (14fl oz) clear apple juice

284g jar no-added-sugar apricot jam (see page 201)

2 tsp kuzu, cornflour or arrowroot (see tip below)

Caster sugar, to taste

Thick cream and toasted flaked almonds, to serve (optional)

1. Put the whole apricots into a pan with the apple juice, keeping back a few tablespoons of the juice. Bring to the boil, cover, then leave to simmer until tender but still plump and whole: 10–15 minutes, but keep checking.

2. Gently drain the apricots, reserving the liquid. Put the apricots on to a serving dish. Pour the liquid back into the pan. Add the apricot jam, and bring to the boil.

3. In a small bowl mix the kuzu, cornflour or arrowroot with the reserved apple juice, add some of the hot liquid from the pan, then tip it into the pan and stir over the heat for a minute or so, to make a slightly thickened glossy glaze.

4. Taste the glaze – and a little piece of apricot – and stir some sugar into the glaze as necessary.

5. Pour and spoon the glaze over and around the apricots. Serve warm or cold, with the cream and toasted almonds, if you like.

Tip: Kuzu is a white lumpy powder extracted from the roots of a wild Japanese plant and is available from Japanese shops and good health shops. It does a similar job to cornflour or arrowroot but makes a particularly clear, smooth, almost jellied sauce or glaze, and (like arrowroot) is said to have a soothing effect on the digestion.

Make it vegan: Substitute soya cream for the dairy cream, or simply serve the compote on its own.

Hot Plum Compote with Cinnamon

This is such a lovely way to prepare plums, in tender, chunky pieces bathed in cinnamon-flavoured juices. I love to use kuzu (see page 197) to thicken the sauce; you can get it at really good Japanese or wholefood shops, do try it if you can get it, otherwise, use cornflour. See if you can also find brown rice syrup in your local wholefood shop; it's a beautiful, natural sweetener that I love to use for this and other desserts, though you could use maple syrup or clear honey.

Serves 4

500g (1lb 2oz) red plums
½ cinnamon stick
Piece of pared lemon zest
400ml (14fl oz) apple juice
A little honey, rice syrup or maple syrup (optional)
2 tbsp kuzu
50g (2oz) blanched almonds (optional)

1. Cut the plums into quarters, discarding the stones.

2. Put the plums into a saucepan with the cinnamon stick and lemon zest. Remove 3–4 tablespoons of the apple juice and set aside. Pour the rest into the pan with the plums and bring to the boil. Let the plums simmer until tender to the point of a knife. This might be in as little as 3 minutes: they cook very quickly – don't let them get soggy! Remove from the heat, taste, and add a little honey, rice syrup or maple syrup if necessary.

3. Tip the plums out of the pan into a colander set over a bowl. Pour the plum liquid back into the pan and bring to the boil.

4. In a small bowl mix the kuzu to a paste with the reserved apple juice, then pour some of the hot plum liquid into the bowl, mix and tip it all into the pan. Stir over the heat for 2–3 minutes. As soon as the liquid thickens to a beautiful clear, glossy sauce, remove the pan from the heat.

5. Transfer the plums to a serving bowl, or put into individual bowls, pour the sauce over, and add the blanched almonds if you're using them. This is beautiful hot, cold or warm; the sauce becomes slightly jellied as the mixture cools.

Tip: You could use bought blanched almonds, but they're never as nice as the ones you prepare yourself. To do this, just boil normal almonds in water for 2 minutes, then drain, rinse under the cold tap and pop the almonds out of their skins with your fingers.

Gooseberry and Elderflower Fool

Such a lovely, classic pudding: one of the real tastes of summer; just thinking about it makes me feel happy! Use a little caster sugar to keep the flavours true, though you could use honey, maple syrup or even agave syrup if you prefer. A delicate almond biscuit makes the perfect accompaniment.

Serves 4

400g (14oz) green gooseberries, topped and tailed

2 tbsp elderflower concentrate

100g (3½oz) golden caster sugar, honey or maple syrup

200ml (7fl oz) double cream

Mint leaves or a few tiny elderflowers, to decorate (optional)

Almond biscuits, to serve

1. Put a shallow dish, large enough to hold the cooked gooseberries, into the freezer, for cooling the gooseberries quickly after they've cooked.

2. Put the gooseberries into a saucepan with the elderflower concentrate and the sugar, cover, and cook gently for about 10 minutes, until the gooseberries have collapsed.

3. If you're going to serve this within the 30 minutes, you'll need to cool the gooseberries quickly, so transfer them to the chilled dish, mash them with a fork or potato masher, and let them cool for as long as you can: they don't need to be ice cold, but cool enough to mix with the cream without curdling it. (I have been known to break all the rules and put the dish of cooked gooseberries in the freezer for a few minutes to help the cooling process!)

4. Whisk the cream until thick, then fold in the cold mashed gooseberries. Heap the mixture into 4 glass bowls, decorate with mint leaves or elderflowers, if using, and serve with almond biscuits alongside.

Jewelled Fruit Flan

A tumble of strawberries, raspberries and blueberries with a shiny golden glaze of apricot jam, in a melt-in-your-mouth flan base – it's stunning. I like using spelt flour pastry but it is quite crumbly in texture so you may prefer a regular shortcrust pastry; either is delicious! You'll need a shallow 20cm (8in) flan tin (no more than 2.5cm (1in) deep). The jam I used is the gorgeous, no-sugar-added one that comes in those tall slim jars, made by St Dalfour, and widely available.

Serves 4

For the pastry

200g (7oz) spelt flour

½ tsp salt

8 tbsp cold-pressed rapeseed oil

2 tbsp water

For the filling

284g jar apricot no-sugar-added jam

150g (5oz) strawberries, halved or quartered as necessary, leafy green part removed

125g (4½oz) blueberries

75g (3oz) raspberries

Thick cream, crème fraîche or strained Greek yoghurt, to serve (optional)

1. Preheat the oven to 200ºC (400ºF), Gas 6.

2. Make the flan case: put the flour and salt into a bowl, pour in the oil and water, and mix gently with a fork until it holds together.

3. Gather the pastry into a ball and roll it out between two pieces of cling film, making the pastry as thin as possible – the cling film really helps here. Give it a half turn every so often, keeping the cling film in place.

4. Peel off the top piece of cling film then invert the pastry over a shallow 20cm (8in) flan tin and press it into place. Peel off the remaining piece of cling film, trim the edges of the pastry and prick the base. Bake for 6–8 minutes, until crisp and lightly browned. Allow it to cool for 5 minutes or so if there's time.

5. Tip the jam into a saucepan and warm over a gentle heat so that it melts a bit, then spoon and lightly spread about half of it over the base of the flan. Tumble the berries on top randomly, all over the flan, then drizzle the rest of the jam over and around them, to make a beautiful, shiny finish. Serve as it is, or with cream or yoghurt.

Make it vegan: Substitute soya cream for the dairy cream, or simply serve the flan without accompaniment.

Mango and Cardamom Fool

Rich, creamy and delectable ... I like to use a really ripe, fragrant mango, then there's no need for additional sweetening.

Serves 4

1 large sweet ripe mango

200ml (7fl oz) double cream

200ml (7fl oz) thick Greek yoghurt

Seeds from 4–6 cardamom pods, crushed

4 sprigs of fresh mint, to decorate

1. Cut the two cheeks of the mango about 5mm (¼in) each side of the stalk; then cut off the peel and cut the flesh into rough pieces.

2. Blend the pieces of mango to a smooth, thick purée.

3. Whip the cream until thick and holding its shape, then gently fold it into the yoghurt.

4. Add the mango purée and the crushed cardamom to the mixture, stirring gently, so that the fool has streaks of gold and white.

5. Heap the mixture into individual serving glasses; garnish with a sprig of fresh mint.

Make it vegan: Use thick, plain, unsweetened soya yoghurt and vegan sour cream, both available from really good health shops.

Warm Figs Braised in Honey with Toasted Almonds

Sweet, unctuous, warm figs with a crunch of golden toasted almonds and some cool thick Greek yoghurt or crème fraîche: this tastes special and luxurious but is simple to make. I like to use a strongly flavoured, thick honey: fair-trade forest honey is my favourite.

Serves 4

8 fresh figs

4 tbsp strongly flavoured honey, such as thyme, fair-trade forest honey

Good pinch of sea salt

50g (2oz) flaked almonds

Thick Greek yoghurt or crème fraîche, to serve

1. Cut a cross in the top of the figs, right through the stem, almost to the base, but keep the pieces joined at the base.

2. Put the honey and pinch of salt into a shallow flameproof casserole and heat gently until it bubbles, then put the figs into the casserole on top of the honey, scooping up some of the honey with a spoon and pouring it over and inside the figs.

3. Cook over a gentle heat for 3–10 minutes, until the figs are warm, and tender. Keep spooning the melted honey over them as they cook, and make sure you remove them from the heat before they get too soft and collapse.

4. While the figs are cooking, put the flaked almonds into a small, dry saucepan and stir over a moderate heat until they turn golden brown and smell toasted. Remove them from the heat immediately, and tip them out of the pan and on to a plate, so they don't go on cooking.

5. Serve the figs in their honey-syrup, topped with toasted almonds, with yoghurt or crème fraîche.

Make it vegan: Use maple syrup instead of honey, and serve with vegan soured cream, which you can get at health shops and some large supermarkets.

Turkish Fruit Salad

A fruit salad with the minimum of preparation, served in Turkey and throughout the Middle East. It makes a stunning finale to a meal if you really go for it and pile up a colourful selection of different fruits on a bed of crushed ice, topping it with halved passion fruit and shiny red pomegranate seeds.

Serves 4

Vegan

4–5 different types of fresh fruit such as watermelon slices, large and luscious strawberries, raspberries, juicy ripe cherries, black grapes, ripe figs, apricots, nectarines

2–3 passion fruits

1 pomegranate

Wedges of lemon or lime and fresh mint leaves, to serve (optional)

1. Prepare the fruit minimally: leave the skin on the watermelon slices, leave the green part on the strawberries, halve or quarter larger fruits such as peaches.

2. Make a bed of crushed ice on a large serving dish and arrange the fruit attractively on top, including the cut passion fruits.

3. Cut the pomegranate in half horizontally and remove the seeds by holding the halves over a bowl, cut side down, and whacking them with a wooden spoon until the seeds fall into the bowl. Scatter over the top of the fruit platter.

4. Decorate with lemon or lime wedges and fresh mint leaves (if using).

Instant Strawberry and Honey Ice Cream

If you've got frozen strawberries in the freezer, cream, honey, and a strong food processor, you really can make this in an instant – and you can even make a very good vegan version too.

Serves 4

450g (1lb) frozen strawberries, straight out of the freezer

4 heaped tbsp honey

568ml (1 pint) single cream

1. Pour all the ingredients into a food processor and whizz until thick and creamy – ice cream, in fact. Serve at once.

Make it vegan: Use soya cream instead of dairy cream, and maple syrup or sugar instead of honey.

Satsuma Syllabub

This makes a luxurious end to a special meal. It's very rich, so serve small portions in wine glasses.

Serves 4

2 large satsumas

175ml (6fl oz) double cream

1 tbsp maple syrup

1. Grate the zest of one of the satsumas into a bowl. Add the cream and leave for 20 minutes, for the flavours to develop.

2. Strain the cream through a nylon sieve into another bowl, pressing through as much oil from the skin as you can.

3. Cut some curls of peel from the unzested satsuma to use as decoration. Squeeze the juice from both satsumas and add to the bowl, along with the maple syrup. Whisk the mixture, gently to prevent curdling, until it is thick and fluffy.

4. Spoon into serving glasses and keep them cold until ready to serve, decorated with the curls of satsuma peel.

Tip: Eat these soon after making them; the mixture may begin to separate after about an hour.

Cinnamon Pancakes with Rose-scented Raspberry Jam

These are special pancakes, light and tender, but made with just flour, chickpea flour and water. Served with the warm, rose-scented jam, they're bliss-on-a-plate!

Serves 4

Vegan

For the pancakes

75g (3oz) chickpea flour

75g (3oz) self-raising flour

300–350ml (11–12fl oz) cold water

Olive oil, for frying

Ground cinnamon, to serve

For the rose-scented jam

284g jar no-added-sugar raspberry jam (see page 201)

2–3 tsp rosewater, or to taste

1. Start with the jam: put it into a small saucepan, along with 2 teaspoons of the rosewater; set over a very low heat to warm through and melt, but don't let it get too hot.

2. To make the pancakes, put the chickpea flour into a bowl and mix with a spoon to break up any lumps, then add the self-raising flour and gradually stir in the water, to make a thin batter.

3. Heat 2 tablespoons olive oil in a wide non-stick frying pan. When it's smoking hot, tip in some batter, swirling the frying pan as you do, so that the batter runs all over the base. This batter doesn't flow in the same way as a conventional batter, so you just need to tip and swirl the pan a bit more than usual to help it to spread thinly over the base.

4. Let the pancake cook for a minute or two. Lift the edges with a spatula to see how it's cooking: it needs to be a deep, golden brown. Then turn it over with a fish slice and cook the other side briefly. Put the pancake on a plate and keep it warm while you make the rest.

5. Check the jam, and add the rest of the rosewater if you want – or even a drop more, depending on how strongly flavoured the rosewater is, and how scented you want the jam to be.

6. Put a little jam on to the centre of a pancake, gently roll it up and dust with cinnamon. Repeat with all the pancakes, and serve. Alternatively serve the pancakes, cinnamon and jam separately, and let everyone help themselves.

Tip: Rosewater varies in strength; the stronger the rosewater, the less you need to use. Alternatively, you could serve these pancakes with rose jam.

Glazed Pears with Crunchy Almond Filling

Tender cooked pear halves with a crunchy almond filling: easy to do, and a bit special. I adapted this recipe from one by Dragana Brown in *The Karma Cookbook*, and it has become one of my favourite desserts.

Serves 4
Vegan

4 large pears
500ml (18fl oz) apple or pear juice
Piece of pared lemon zest
Pinch of salt
8 tsp maple syrup

For the filling
100g (3½oz) ground almonds
2 tbsp rice syrup, light or dark (see tip); or maple syrup

For the glaze
4–6 tsp kuzu or cornflour (see tip on page 197)
2 tbsp lemon juice
1 tsp grated lemon zest

1. Halve the pears, leaving the stalks intact. Thinly peel the pears and carefully scoop out the cores: a teaspoon is good for this.

2. Put the pears into a saucepan, add all but a few tablespoons of the apple or pear juice (set this aside for later), the lemon zest and salt. Bring to the boil, then reduce the heat, cover and simmer for 5–7 minutes, or until the pears are tender when pierced with the point of a knife.

3. Meanwhile, make the filling: dry-fry the almonds in a frying pan for about 3 minutes, or until they smell toasty and start to turn golden – tip them out of the pan on to a plate the moment this stage is reached. Put the rice syrup into the frying pan and heat, then put the almonds back in and stir for a minute or two until the mixture thickens. Remove from the heat.

4. When the pears are tender, remove with a slotted spoon and put them on a serving dish. Pour 1 teaspoon of maple syrup into each, then fill the centre generously with the almond mixture.

5. To make the glaze, reheat the cooking liquid. Dissolve 4 teaspoons of the kuzu or cornflour in the reserved apple or pear juice and stir this into the pan; heat gently, stirring, for 2–3 minutes, until thick and clear. If it's not quite thick enough, dissolve the remaining kuzu or cornflour in a couple of tablespoons of water and add that; stir over the heat again. Pour the glaze over and around the pears. Serve hot, warm or cold.

Tip: Rice syrup is a gentle form of sweetening that I think is delicious. You can find it in jars in Japanese shops or really good wholefood or macrobiotic shops. There is a dark – malt – version and a light one: either is fine.

Fruit Salad with Lime and Mint in a Mango Coulis

This is so refreshing, a delicious blend of flavours and textures: crisp, slightly sharp apples, kiwi fruits and sweet grapes, bathed in the sweet fragrance of ripe mango, with an accent of lime and fresh mint ... bliss, and so easy to do.

Serves 4

Vegan

For the fruit salad

2 large russet or other slightly sharp apples, peeled, cored and cut into chunky pieces

4 kiwi fruits, peeled, quartered and cut into chunky pieces

300g (11oz) seedless black grapes

Zest and juice of 2 limes

Maple syrup (optional)

4 sprigs of fresh mint, to serve

For the coulis

1 large ripe mango, or 2 smaller ones

1. To make the fruit salad, mix all the fruits together. Add the lime zest and juice. Taste, and sweeten with a little maple syrup as necessary.

2. To make the coulis, cut the two cheeks of the mango about 5mm (¼in) each side of the stalk; then cut off the peel and cut the flesh into rough pieces. Blend the pieces of mango to a smooth, thick purée.

3. Pour the mango purée into a serving bowl, heap the fruit salad on top and decorate with the mint.

Chocolate Amaretti Pudding

This quick chocolate pudding consists of a crunchy biscuit base with a light, creamy chocolate topping. You can eat it almost immediately or leave it overnight – it gets better all the time. It's a useful emergency pudding because the ingredients are so simple, but you do need to use good-quality plain chocolate.

Serves 4–6

300g (11oz) plain chocolate
  (minimum 50% cocoa solids)
25g (1oz) butter
125g (4½oz) amaretti biscuits
200ml (7fl oz) single cream
½ tsp finely grated orange zest
Strands of orange zest, to decorate

1. First make a start on the topping: break 200g (7oz) of the chocolate into pieces and put them into a deep bowl set over a pan of steaming water. Leave until the chocolate has melted, then remove the bowl from the pan and stand it in a bowl of cold water to cool it down quickly.

2. While the chocolate is melting, make the base, but first draw a potato peeler down the length of the remaining chocolate to make a few chocolate curls for decorating the pudding: keep these on one side. Break the rest of the chocolate into pieces, put them into a medium saucepan with the butter and melt over a very low heat.

3. Crush the amaretti biscuits, then remove the chocolate mixture from the heat and stir in the biscuit crumbs until they are well coated.

4. Put a 20cm (8in) plain flan ring on a plate and spoon the crumb mixture into it, pressing it down firmly with the back of a spoon. Put it in a cool place (I put mine in the freezer).

5. Now pour the cream into the bowl of melted chocolate, add the grated orange zest and whisk until thick and pale. This will only take a few minutes if the mixture is cold enough: if it takes longer, put it in the fridge or freezer for a few minutes.

6. Spoon the chocolate cream on to the base, taking it right to the edges and smoothing the top with the back of the spoon. You can serve it almost immediately or refrigerate it. Run a knife around the edges and remove the flan ring, neatening the edges with the knife – the longer you leave it the easier it will be to turn out. Decorate the top with the reserved chocolate curls and the orange strands before serving. It's nice as it is, or with some extra single cream, or with cream lightly whipped with 1 tablespoon of rum, brandy or Amaretto.

Make it vegan: Make sure the chocolate you use is vegan: many, but not all, types of plain chocolate are. Use soya cream instead of dairy cream, and crunchy vegan biscuits instead of amaretti biscuits, and make it with, or without, the orange, depending on the flavour of the biscuits you choose: you could decorate with flaked almonds or chopped stem ginger instead.

Grilled Pineapple with Brown Sugar, Rum and Crème Fraîche

Wedges of grilled pineapple, with their leaves still attached, look quite dramatic, and they taste wonderful, because grilling intensifies the pineapple flavour.

Serves 4

1 large, juicy pineapple

A little flavourless cooking oil, such as grapeseed or light olive oil

About 6 tbsp soft brown sugar

6 tbsp rum

Crème fraîche, to serve

1. Cut the pineapple down through the leaves, slicing it into eighths.

2. Brush both sides of each piece of pineapple lightly with oil and coat with the soft brown sugar.

3. Put the pieces of pineapple on to a grill pan and grill until the sugar has melted and the pineapple has lightly browned, but don't let the sugar burn, then turn the pieces over and repeat with the second side.

4. Put the pieces of pineapple on plates and pour the rum over them. Serve with crème fraîche.

Tip: Make sure the rum you use is vegetarian or vegan-friendly: this is not difficult to find.

Fast White Chocolate and Lime Cheesecake

A stunning, beautiful cheesecake you can make in less than 30 minutes. Perfect just as it is, but if you want to add a contrasting colour and a flavour that really complements it, try serving it with Mango Coulis (see page 214).

Serves 6–8

200g (7oz) white chocolate, broken into pieces

200g (7oz) digestive biscuits, crushed

1 tsp ground ginger

75g (3oz) soft butter

200g (7oz) medium cream cheese

300ml (11fl oz) double cream (not 'extra thick')

Finely grated zest of 1 lime, with extra strands to decorate

2 tbsp freshly squeezed lime juice

1. Put the white chocolate into a bowl set over a pan of steaming water; leave for 4–5 minutes until the chocolate has melted.

2. Meanwhile, mix the crushed biscuits with the ginger and butter, then press this into a 20cm (8in) springform cake tin.

3. Beat the cream cheese in a bowl until creamy; in another bowl, whisk the cream until it stands in peaks; get it as firm as you can, but don't let it start to break up.

4. Gently stir the melted white chocolate into the cream cheese, along with the grated lime zest and juice, then gently fold in the whipped cream.

5. Tip the mixture on top of the crumb crust and smooth gently to level.

6. This can be served straight away – it will be soft and creamy but firm enough to cut into slices. If you put it in the fridge for a few minutes it will become a bit firmer and easier to slice, and it's still delicious after 24 hours in the fridge.

Speedy Chocolate and Hazelnut Brownies

You can just make these in 30 minutes as long as you have all the ingredients prepared in advance, and use a shallow tin, such as a Swiss roll tin, for cooking them, rather than a deeper one. If you make them in a deeper tin, allow a few more minutes in the oven. They're delicious served warm with vanilla ice cream. My favourite brown sugars to use for these are muscovado or rapadura, as they're the least processed. You can get them at health shops or many supermarkets.

Makes 15

100g (3½oz) plain chocolate, broken into pieces

100g (3½oz) butter, in rough pieces

225g (8oz) dark brown sticky sugar

2 large or 3 medium eggs

50g (2oz) self-raising flour

125g (4½oz) skinned, lightly toasted hazelnuts, roughly chopped

1. Preheat the oven to 190°C (375°F), Gas 5. Line a Swiss roll tin with a piece of baking parchment.

2. Put the chocolate and butter into a pan. Stir over the heat until melted; be careful not to let the mixture burn.

3. Remove from the heat and stir in the sugar, then the eggs and flour. Beat together until smooth.

4. Stir in the hazelnuts, then pour into the tin and bake for about 25 minutes, or until firm at the edges and still soft in the middle. Cool for a few minutes, then cut into slices and remove from the tin with a spatula.

Chocolate 'Truffles' and 'Power Balls'

Medjool dates are the big squishy ones you can get with the fresh fruit in some supermarkets, or maybe with the dried fruit … they're in between fresh and dried, and usually come in a rather fancy transparent container. If you can't get them, you could use ordinary dates, but soak them first in boiling water for about 15 minutes to soften them.

Makes about 12 of each type

Vegan

For the date and chocolate 'truffles'

6 medjool dates (or 8 normal dates), stones removed

85g almond butter

2 tbsp cocoa powder

½ tsp real vanilla extract

Extra cocoa powder for dusting

12 paper bonbon cases

For the apricot, almond and cardamom 'power balls'

100g (3½oz) soft apricots without added sulphur dioxide (they'll probably be organic)

100g (3½oz) ground almonds

1 tsp real vanilla extract

Seeds from 4 cardamom pods, crushed

2–3 tbsp ground almonds, to coat

12 blanched almonds, to decorate

1. To make the date and chocolate 'truffles', put the dates into a food processor with the almond butter, cocoa powder and vanilla extract, and blitz to a smooth paste. Alternatively, put them into a deep bowl or goblet and use a hand-held blender.

2. Have ready a piece of baking parchment sprinkled with a little cocoa powder. Divide the sticky mixture into about 12 pieces and roll in the cocoa powder. Place in bonbon cases. They will become firmer as they dry out slightly.

3. For the apricot, almond and cardamom power balls, just blitz together, in a food processor or with a hand-held blender, the apricots, ground almonds, vanilla and cardamom, to make a stiff, sticky mixture.

4. Form the mixture into 12 balls, roll them in ground almonds, and stick a blanched almond in the top of each to decorate.

Tips: Natural dried apricots, the kind without sulphur dioxide added to preserve the colour, are dark brown, with a gorgeous rich, almost molasses-like flavour.

I love the hint of cardamom in the power balls; it gives them an exotic, Middle Eastern flavour, but a plainer version, without this, is also very good and children sometimes prefer it.

Chocolate Chestnut Cake

This is a wonderfully rich cake, like a fantastic chocolate torte. You can easily make it in 30 minutes, but the longer you wait to serve it, the firmer and more sliceable it will become. It makes enough for a 500g (1lb) loaf tin. You can also make a sandwich cake version – double the quantities and bake in two round 17.5cm (7in) cake tins, then sandwich together with fresh whipped cream.

Serves 6

150g (5oz) plain chocolate (70% cocoa solids), broken into pieces

435g tin unsweetened chestnut purée

90g (3oz) soft butter

4 tbsp maple syrup

150ml (5fl oz) double cream, whipped, to serve

1. Put the chocolate into a bowl set over a pan of gently steaming water and leave for a few minutes to melt.

2. Beat together the chestnut purée, butter and maple syrup, then beat in the melted chocolate.

3. Line a 500g (1lb) shallow loaf tin with baking parchment to cover the base and sides. Spoon the chocolate mixture into the tin and level the top.

4. The cake firms up quickly, and if you're careful you can turn it out, strip off the paper, and slice it straight away, but the longer it waits, the firmer and more sliceable it gets, especially if you put it into the fridge. Serve with whipped cream.

Quick Almond and Raspberry Biscuits

These are very quick to make and become crisp as they cool (don't try eating them straight from the oven because the jam will be boiling hot). They're made from natural, healthy ingredients and aren't too sweet, so I feel perfectly happy giving them to my grandchildren, and they love making them with me, too. The biscuits are also lovely made with apricot jam.

Makes 18

Vegan

200g (7oz) wholemeal spelt flour

200g (7oz) ground almonds

Pinch of salt

¼–½ tsp cinnamon (optional)

6 tbsp cold-pressed rapeseed oil

6 tbsp real maple syrup

About 3 tbsp no-added-sugar raspberry and/or apricot jam (see page 201)

1. Preheat the oven to 180ºC (350ºF), Gas 4. Line a baking sheet with baking parchment.

2. Put the flour, almonds, salt and cinnamon, if you're using it, into a bowl. Add the rapeseed oil and maple syrup to the bowl and mix gently, to form a soft dough.

3. Divide the dough into 18 pieces, roll each into a ball, then put them on to the baking sheet and flatten them a bit with the palm of your hand. Make an indentation in the centre of each with your fingertip, and fill this with jam.

4. Bake in the preheated oven for 15–20 minutes, or until golden brown: we prefer them golden and tender, rather than darker and firmer; they will become crisper as they cool on a wire rack.

Tips: If you love the flavour of almonds, you can intensify it by adding a drop or two of real almond extract.

People who are sensitive to wheat often find that they can eat spelt flour – it's made from an early variety before wheat was hybridised – but these also work well made with barley flour, which is gorgeous, if you can find it.

Banana with Macadamia 'Salted Caramel' Sauce

I love using ingredients in unusual ways to create unexpected flavours. Here, I've whizzed macadamia nuts with maple syrup, coconut milk, vanilla and a pinch of salt to create a creamy topping that to me tastes like smooth, rich, salted caramel, and it's gorgeous over bananas. See what you think!

Serves 4

Vegan

4 bananas

Roasted salted macadamia nuts, crushed, to serve

For the 'salted caramel' sauce

100g (3½oz) unsalted macadamia nuts

½ tsp sea salt

4 tbsp coconut milk from a tin

6 tbsp maple syrup

½ tsp vanilla extract

1. To make the sauce, put everything into a blender and whizz until thick and creamy. The more powerful your blender, the smoother and creamier your sauce will be: keep blending until you get it as smooth as you can.

2. Peel and slice the bananas, divide between 4 individual dishes, pour the sauce over the top, sprinkle with a few crushed salted macadamias, and serve.

Index

Egyptian rice and lentils with
caramelised onions and pine nuts 87
onion bhajees 63
red onion tarts 138
orange-scented bulgur pilaf 150

P

pak choy
black sesame-coated tofu triangles
with noodles and pak choy 111
red hot udon stir-fry 108
pancakes
cinnamon pancakes with rose-scented
raspberry jam 212
quick dosa masala 120
pappardelle with wild mushrooms 144
parsnips
creamy parsnip soup 15
crunchy roast parsnips with
horseradish dip 186
pasta
broad bean lasagne 77
macaroni cheese 83
pappardelle with wild mushrooms 144
quick Mediterranean pasta 79
spaghetti alla puttanesca 80
spaghetti with lentil bolognaise 82
spinach tagliatelle with walnuts 141
wholemeal penne with broccoli and
pesto 78
pastries
little goat's cheese filo parcels 28
Mediterranean strudel 154–6
spanakopita with tzatziki 68
pastry, walnut 99
pâté, nut 58
pears
Asian pear salad 23
glazed pears with crunchy almond
filling 213
peas
bulgur, edamame, pea and broad
bean salad 41
French-style petit pois 181
green pea and mint soup 19
oven-baked asparagus and pea risotto 88
petits pois and mint omelette topping 57
pecans
almond and pecan roast 149
penne
quick Mediterranean pasta 79
wholemeal penne with broccoli
and pesto 78
peppers
griddled courgette and red pepper rice
bowls 147–8

grilled halloumi skewers with red and
yellow peppers 134
grilling 156
Mediterranean strudel 154–6
pepper omelette topping 57
pointed red peppers stuffed with artichoke
hearts and feta 128
quick Mediterranean pasta 79
red hot udon stir-fry 108
red pepper salsa 29
Thai-flavoured chickpea and millet cakes
with red pepper sauce 107
ultimate red bean chilli 93
pesto
tomato and pesto tart 99
wholemeal penne with broccoli and pesto 78
petits pois *see* peas
pilaf
orange-scented bulgur pilaf 150
wonderful rice pilaf 152
pine nuts
Egyptian rice and lentils with caramelised
onions and pine nuts 87
griddled Mediterranean vegetables with
couscous, hummus and toasted pine
nuts 129
quinoa with basil and pine nuts 46
warm butternut squash with baby-leaf
spinach, red onion and pine nuts 51
pineapple
grilled pineapple with brown sugar,
rum and crème fraîche 217
pizzas, French bread 101
plums
hot plum compote with cinnamon 199
pomegranate
pomegranate raita 152
Turkish fruit salad 209
warm quinoa salad with broad beans
and pomegranate 44
potatoes
avocado and roasted potato salad 54
Bircher potatoes 188
Bombay potatoes 122–3
gratin Dauphinois 137
potato and celeriac mash 142–4
potato and leek gratin 72
quick dosa masala 120
roast potato wedges with sea salt and
balsamic vinegar 190
rösti 130–2
rösti potato 'crisps' 67
tandoori potato skewers 62
purple sprouting broccoli with gomasio 172

Acknowledgements

Many people have brought their talent and expertise to create this book and I'd like to thank them all so much.

Thank you to Lizzy Gray for inviting me to write it and her splendid editorial team, Elen Jones and George Atsiaris, also Mari Roberts, my excellent copy editor, for all their wonderful input, ideas and guidance; brilliant photographer Myles New, for the stunning food photographs; Annie Hudson, food stylist, and Danny McGuire and Rachel Wood, her assistants, for cooking the recipes so beautifully. Thank you too to Polly Webb-Wilson for the prop styling, Ben Gardiner for the great book design and Heike Schuessler for the cover.
  I'd also like to thank my agent, Barbara Levy, for her advice and help, and my dear husband and family who are always there for me.

My love and gratitude to them all.

To vegetarians, would-be vegetarians
and vegans everywhere, with my love.

First published in 2012 by Collins

HarperCollins Publishers
77–85 Fulham Palace Road
London W6 8JB

www.harpercollins.co.uk

16 15 14 13 12
9 8 7 6 5 4 3 2 1

Text © Rose Elliot 2012
Photography © Myles New 2012

Rose Elliot asserts her moral right to be
identified as the author of this work.

A catalogue record for this book is available
from the British Library.

ISBN: 9780007458271

Food Stylist: Annie Hudson
Prop Stylist: Polly Webb-Wilson

Printed and bound in China by
South China Printing Co Ltd.